P9-BIO-510

BRIEF OUTLINE ON THE STUDY OF THEOLOGY

Friedrich Schleiermacher

Translated, with Introductions and Notes by Terrence N. Tice

JOHN KNOX PRESS
ATLANTA

A translation of Friedrich Schleiermacher's *Kurze Darstellung des theologischen Studiums zum Behuf einleitender Vorlesungen* (Berlin, 1830).

Third printing 1977

ISBN 0-8042-0485-3
LIBRARY OF CONGRESS CATALOG CARD NUMBER: 66-10301

PRINTED IN THE UNITED STATES OF AMERICA

PREFACE

Schleiermacher is justly known as "the father of modern theology." The outline of theological studies which he prepared for his students shows why better than any other single work. His 1799 *Addresses on Religion* has probably been the most influential popular discussion on the nature of religion in modern times, displaying as it does the relation of religion to the whole of human life. His systematic statement of Christian doctrine in *The Christian Faith,* which appeared over twenty years later, presented the first great sustained definition of Christian belief since the Reformation. In the way it fastens on God's decisive action for man in Christ, in the attention it pays to the current experience of the Church, in the cultured, scholarly insight it lays bare, and in the irenic care it exemplifies throughout, *The Christian Faith* remains a model for all subsequent attempts in its genre. It is the simple, down-to-business *Brief Outline* of 1811 and 1830, however, which best shows the fertilizing effect of his labors, for this outline presents the whole of theology in a cohesive manner never before achieved, while also preserving the basic outlook of the other two books.

By design, the final revision of all three books appeared in 1830-1831. With the present edition of the *Brief Outline,* the famous interlocking triad is made available to the general reader for the first time in English translation.

This can become an important book for any intelligent Christian who wants to take responsible leadership in the life of the Church. For here Schleiermacher presents his views of what Christian theology is and of how the work of theology can be seen as a whole. The book describes the personal vision of a great scholar; it was conceived at a particular juncture in the Church's history, and organized to meet the needs of the Church in early nineteenth century Germany. Without question, its message has to be rethought now and adapted to new circumstances. Its continuing importance, however, lies not only in the historic role it has played but also in the remarkably direct relevance it still has for our own situation.

Schleiermacher would have welcomed contemporary laymen among the "students of theology" for whom he wrote, for many now assume the sort of leadership which he would have applauded but which was virtually closed to laymen in his own day. He shows throughout this book that he was sensitive to the layman's built-in skepticism both as to whether theology is practicable and as to whether, in the end, one can make sense out of theology at all. He does not, however, fall for the lure here of oversimplifying the state of affairs only to gain an easy but pointless consent. Instead, he tries first to get to the heart of the matter and then to let all its complexity unfold according to need. Consistent with his own style of life, he counsels patience before the enormous demands laid upon theology taken as a total discipline, but courage before the task of learning what one needs to know. He helps by presenting an ordered perspective over the whole field, poking at the details wherever they appear especially significant. On this basis the "student"—whether professional theologian, perplexed pastor, or curious layman—is invited to develop his own understanding of the matter afresh. Schleiermacher is not a take-it-or-leave-it teacher. He is a partner in dialogue. He merits our considered response simply because he has laid the foundations of our common discourse so well.

Much of what Schleiermacher had to say has become our common heritage in the Church, and to no small degree through his actual stimulus. Insofar as this little book presents a fresh challenge even now, and not only a survey over familiar ground, it may help us make up our own minds about what theology ought to be and encourage some of us to do theology accordingly. Even though the challenge does not always come in terms we would ordinarily use, its substance is crystal clear. In sum, the challenge is to view theology as servant to the Church's mission in the contemporary world. Even once we have temporarily laid aside the specialized demands of theology, we are thus still confronted in a striking way with the whole problem of what it means to be a thinking Christian.

The translation follows the critical edition of Heinrich Scholz (Leipzig, 1910), which includes both the greatly revised text of 1830 and the original edition of 1811. Very few alterations after 1811 show a change either in Schleiermacher's general outlook or in his organization of the material. In several places, however, the 1811 text has been referred to in the notes, for clarification. The first English translation of the 1830 edition, by William Farrer, has also been compared: *Brief Outline of the Study of Theology* (Edinburgh: T & T Clark, 1850, xvi, 220 pp.). One must give tribute to the responsible piece of work done by this English congregationalist over a century ago. It is now nevertheless irretrievably out-of-date, for Schleiermacher's language is extremely precise and compact, and most important historical and interpretative material necessary for understanding it in depth was not yet available in 1850.

No attempt has been made to supply additional material or bibliography on the hundreds of subjects mentioned. This can be better done by consulting current sources in the field. Some helps for understanding the text have been provided, through introductions and notes. The table of contents and a full index have also been affixed for this purpose. The headings in the main text are Schleiermacher's own. Material in parentheses is his, that in brackets or footnotes has been added by the editor.

Since in many respects Schleiermacher's book *The Christian Faith* is a companion to this one, references to it have been supplied wherever relevant. These are cited according to paragraph, subparagraph, and page (CF 19:1,88f). Pages are also cited from the *Addresses on Religion* (Addr. 237) and the *Soliloquies,* and from the collected works, *Sämmtliche Werke* (SW III.9,816). Further cross-references are given, in addition to Schleiermacher's own. In view of the highly systematic character of the outline and the author's great economy of statement, these are often important in order to clarify his meaning.

Care has been taken to give Schleiermacher's expression an authentically contemporary form without sacrificing the rigorous, exact movement of his thought. Wherever called for, translation of key terms has followed his own consistent usage.

The reader can get a useful grasp of the book's structure—and probably save himself both time and needless perplexity—by first looking at the general introduction and table of contents and then skimming through the whole, including the editorial postscript, which briefly discusses each major section, before attempting to follow the book through from start to finish. It is a thin book, but it covers a territory so large one is always in danger of getting lost in it. Schleiermacher has provided a good typographical map of the territory here, one made-to-order for the traveler weary of elaborate guidebooks which dwell on the minutiae of theology but fail to reveal its great contours. That person will be well repaid who takes care to master the map before venturing too far into the territory.

Terrence N. Tice
Geneva, Switzerland
April 1965

CONTENTS

EDITOR'S GENERAL INTRODUCTION

The short definition of theology given in the very first paragraph of this outline sets the tone for the whole book. It also shows where Schleiermacher contributes most decisively to current debate over what theology ought to be. "Theology," he says, "is a positive science, whose parts join into a cohesive whole only through their common relation to a particular mode of faith, i.e., a particular way of being conscious of God." The entire outline is about this definition. Three features of the definition stand out, though, and these are best explained in terms of §§ 2-19 of *The Christian Faith*.

1. First, theology is a "positive science." By "positive" Schleiermacher means studies which are not merely empirical or speculative or theoretical in character but rather (a) refer directly to actual historical experience, (b) within a given social relationship, and (c) in order to serve a definite practical function. The positive reference of Christian theology is to the "particular way of being conscious of God" found in the historical experience of Christianity. Its practical aim is, purely and simply, to provide for apt, effective leadership in the Christian Church. Other ways of talking about God may be interesting, but they are not theology.

Theology is "science" in that by using rational and orderly methods it assembles a particular kind of knowledge, which can be validated in experience. It is not a segment of general science, because it refers to actions of God inexplicable on purely natural grounds (see CF § 13:P.S.). Nor is it even part of a supposed "science of religion." Schleiermacher holds that religious consciousness is a universal element in human nature. At the same time, he denies that a formula for "natural religion" can be extracted from all religious experiences. Even if it were thought that such a formula had been extracted, he argues, it would only in fact represent the peculiar views of individuals. No formula for "natural religion" could ever circumscribe the actual experience of a religious community or even successfully serve as the basis for one (see CF § 10:P.S.).

For Schleiermacher, the science called theology takes its place within the whole of human learning, just as religion can both draw upon and affect the whole of human experience. Because Christianity has gained historical prominence and embraces a vast expanse of human culture, Christian thought naturally stands under the rubric that "everything is to be understood in the fullness of its relations" (§ 184). That is to say, all the proper subject matter and language of Christian thought is to be understood both historically and scientifically in the fullest, broadest sense of these words. Its substance is not isolated from any part of human experience. On the other hand, just as religion has its own distinctive character, and takes on special features in every religious community, so theology likewise maintains its own distinctive subject matter and language. Neither the subject matter nor the language is ever strictly determinable from the nontheological disciplines. From a Christian viewpoint, the necessity for theological science comes not from any general type of experience whatever, nor even from any general type of ideas about God, but from the specific historical "given" of Christianity itself.

As a student of Christian theology, therefore, you do not start with man or God, in Schleiermacher's view, but with a relationship between God and man which has actually happened. You take an "interest" in this relationship insofar as you have already begun to take part in it within the life of the Christian community. This must be true, Schleiermacher insists, whether you are trying to do exegesis, or Church history, or philosophical theology, or Christian social ethics. Start with a preconceived idea of God, no matter where you got it—whether from an analytic philosopher or from a great theologian—and you are almost sure to go wrong. The same is the case if you start with some general view about "human existence."

2. The second feature which must be stressed is that theological studies attain cohesiveness insofar as the strictly ecclesial and scientific interests which constitute them are joined together (see CF § 17). This reminder is repeated over and over again throughout Schleiermacher's outline, as references given in the index will show. Its importance cannot be overemphasized. Although every individual has to work out his own basic theology, he is able to do so without floundering and without falling into serious error only insofar as he has learned to enter into the

corporate reality of Christianity, on the one hand, and to exercise critical discretion in forming judgments, on the other. Otherwise he is likely to run into all kinds of situations injurious to his own faith, and the map of Christian concerns which Schleiermacher depicts here will soon seem like alien territory.

3. The third main feature of Schleiermacher's outlook is that every theological discipline may be regarded as a contribution to the Church's understanding of the essence, or the distinctive nature, of Christianity. (Again, this notion can be pulled together by referring to passages noted in the index.) The general form of this understanding, as compared with the nature of other religious communities and their faith, is supplied largely through what he calls "philosophical theology." The norm of this understanding is largely clarified through the series of historical studies which begins with "exegetical theology," continues with "Church history," and ends with "historical knowledge of the present condition of Christianity" (current doctrine, ethics, and "statistics"). The application of this understanding for Church leadership is contained in "practical theology."

The whole of Christian theology is contained in these three overlapping areas. All three focus upon the one central fact of "the redemption accomplished by Jesus of Nazareth" (CF § 11). Every theological definition of Christianity, no matter what form it takes or through how many hundreds of pages of exegesis or ethics, history or educational theory, it extends, must take its bearing on that one distinctive historical fact and serve to display its implications for the past or present or future life of the Christian Church. This fact cannot be encapsulated in neat propositional form—though it is perhaps best summed up, for Schleiermacher, in John 1:14. Consequently, no formal deduction can be made from it. Yet the fact remains, and the whole of theology centers upon it: ". . . the Word was made flesh, and dwelt among us . . . and we have beheld his glory. . . ."

Terrence N. Tice

PREFACE TO THE FIRST EDITION

I have always found it extremely difficult to conduct academic lectures by following the outline of someone else's textbook. Every difference of opinion seems immediately to require one to depart from an order of treatment which has issued from another viewpoint. Of course, the more the particular views of people on details are subordinated to a common viewpoint, i.e., the more what is called a school obtains, the easier it becomes to use such a procedure. But everyone knows how little this is the case in theology at present. For the same reason, therefore, which makes it necessary for me to draw up my own scheme—if one is to be used at all, which is certainly advantageous—I am in no position to claim that other teachers should use it. Thus, when it seems rather excessive to publish at large what is only prepared for the use of my students, I console myself with the thought that since these few pages, however constituted, contain my entire present outlook on theological study, perhaps they may stimulate concern by their divergence from other positions and serve to generate something better.

Others customarily include in their courses on encyclopedia a précis of the various disciplines treated. To me it has seemed more suitable to follow those who prefer to direct their students' full attention to matters of form, so that they may better apprehend the significance of the particular parts and of their interrelation.

Dr. Friedrich Schleiermacher
Berlin, December 1810

PREFACE TO THE SECOND EDITION

It is nearly twenty years now since this little book first appeared. Thus, it was perhaps only natural that I should find much to alter in respect to details, even though the viewpoint and the mode of treatment have on the whole remained the same throughout. I hope that alterations in expression and approach have made an improvement, and that the brief explanatory paragraphs attached to the main propositions may not fail of their purpose, which is to make things easier for the reader.

Since numbering the paragraphs of each section separately in the first edition made citations cumbersome, this procedure has been changed.

Dr. Friedrich Schleiermacher
Berlin, October 1830

INTRODUCTION

§ 1. Theology is a positive science, whose parts join into a cohesive whole only through their common relation to a particular mode of faith,[1] i.e., a particular way of being conscious of God. Thus, the various parts of Christian theology belong together only by virtue of their relation to "Christianity."[2] This is the sense in which the word "theology" will always be used here.

Generally speaking, a positive science is an assemblage of scientific elements which belong together not because they form a constituent part of the organization of the sciences, as though by some necessity arising out of the notion of science itself, but only insofar as they are requisite for carrying out a practical task.

Reference is certainly also made to the God of whom we are conscious in the case of "rational theologies" formerly constructed within the organization of sciences. As speculative science, however, these are entirely different from the theology whose definition we are elaborating here.[3]

§ 2. Whether any given mode of faith will give shape to a definite theology depends on the degree to which it is communicated by means of ideas rather than symbolic actions, and likewise on the degree to which it attains historical importance and autonomy.[4] Theologies, moreover, may differ according to every particular mode of faith, in that they correspond to the distinctiveness of each both in content and in form.

A real theology will develop only on the two conditions stated. For, in the first instance, no need for one will arise in a community of small extent; and in the second, where a preponderance of symbolic actions exists the ritual which interprets these hardly deserves to be called a science.

1. In the first edition, *Religion* was the term used. As a synonym for faith it had since gone out of favor, whereupon he used "piety" or "faith."

2. Not "Christendom" *(Christenheit)*, a term he almost never used; see index.

3. Schleiermacher intended the definition of theology in these paragraphs to be compared with that in *The Christian Faith* (=CF), especially §§ 2-19. The point about "rational theology" (=speculative or natural theology) is extremely important; see CF §§ 2:1; 3:4; 19:P.S., and compare § 226 below. Other important points in these introductory paragraphs have been interpreted in the General Introduction above.

4. The first edition added: "i.e., is formed as a Church." See CF §§ 2-6.

§ 3. Theology is not the special responsibility of everyone who belongs to a particular Church, except as they take part in the leadership of the Church. Consequently, we can say that the contrast between leaders and ordinary members and the rise to prominence of theology mutually condition each other.

The expression "leadership of the Church" is meant to be regarded in the broadest sense here, without restriction to any one particular form.

§ 4. The more the Church advances in its growth, and the more linguistic and cultural areas it includes, the more complicated the organization of theology becomes. Christian theology, on this account, has become the most extensively cultivated of all.

The more these two factors enter into the picture, the more numerous are the different ideas and ways of living which theology must take into account, and the more diverse are the historical data to which it must refer.

§ 5. Christian theology, accordingly, is that assemblage of scientific knowledge and practical instruction without the possession and application of which a united leadership of the Christian Church, i.e., a government of the Church in the fullest sense, is not possible.

This is precisely the relation set forth in § 1. [It is important to point out this "positive" relation of theology,] for the Christian faith, in and of itself, does not absolutely require such an apparatus for its effectiveness either within the individual soul or within the relationships which make up the common life of a family.

§ 6. When this same knowledge is acquired and possessed without relation to the "government" of the Church, it ceases to be theological and devolves to those sciences to which it belongs according to its varied content.

Depending on the subject matter, such knowledge would be referred to linguistic and historical studies, psychology and ethics, together with general studies on various sorts of technique and philosophy of religion —two disciplines which are based on psychology and ethics.

§ 7. By virtue of this relation, that same manifold of knowledge is as integrally related to the will to be effective in the leadership of the Church as the body is to the soul.

Without this will, the unity of theology disappears, and its parts decompose into its various elements.

§ 8. However, just as that multifarious knowledge is combined into a theological whole only in the service of a definite interest in Christianity, so this interest in Christianity can likewise only manifest itself appropriately by assimilating that knowledge.

In accordance with § 2, the function of leadership in the Church can only be adequately performed on the basis of a highly developed consciousness of history. At the same time, its true success rests upon a clear knowledge concerning the relationship of the religious aspects of man's life to all the rest.[5]

§ 9. If one should imagine both a religious interest and a scientific spirit conjoined in the highest degree and with the finest balance for the purpose of theoretical and practical activity alike, that would be the idea of a "prince of the Church."

This nomenclature for the theological ideal would, of course, be strictly applicable only when the disparity between such a person and his fellow members in the Church is very great, and where it is possible for him to influence a large part of the Church. It does seem more suitable than the term "Church father," which is already used for a special category of men. Furthermore, its denotation is not in the least restricted to an official position, as such.

§ 10. If one thinks of this balance as having broken down, then the one who has primarily cultivated the knowledge of Christianity is a theologian, in the narrower sense; and, on the contrary, the one who has primarily cultivated activity which pertains to Church government is a clergyman.[6]

This natural separation is more in evidence at certain times and places than at others. The more it prevails, however, the less can the Church subsist without a vital interchange between the two.

Hereafter, the term "theologian" will normally be used in the broader sense, which comprehends both tendencies.

---

5. Compare §§ 21-22; 48; 167; 173. In the CF, only civil government is taken up as a special topic (§ 3:1 and § 105; see index here), although the whole treatment there, as here, rests upon a keen awareness of "the relationship of the religious aspects of man's life to all the rest." One must go to the *Addresses on Religion* (=Addr.) to find outright expression of this awareness, and to his lectures on Christian ethics and practical theology, his ten volumes of sermons, and his many nontheological writings.

6. Compare § 270 and context.

§ 11. Every treatment of theological subjects as such, whatever their nature, stands always within the province of Church leadership; and however the activity of Church leadership may be considered, whether in a more constructive or in a more regulative fashion, this kind of thinking likewise always belongs within the purview of theology in the narrower sense.

Even the especially scientific work of the theologian must aim at promoting the Church's welfare, and is thereby clerical; and even those technical regulations for essentially clerical activities belong within the circle of the theological sciences.

§ 12. If, accordingly, all true theologians also participate in the leadership of the Church, and all who are active in Church government live also within the theological arena, it follows that both an ecclesial interest and a scientific spirit must be united in each person, despite any tendency to lean toward the one side or the other.

If the opposite were the case, then the scholar would no longer be a theologian; he would merely be engaged in working over various theological subjects in the spirit of whatever particular science is proper to them. Likewise, the clergyman's activity would lack both the skill and the foresight of good leadership, degenerating into a mere muddle of attempted influence.

§ 13. Everyone who finds himself called to exercise leadership in the Church discovers the function he is to perform according to the measure in which one or the other of these two elements is dominant within him.

Without such an inner calling, no one is truly either a theologian or a clergyman. Neither of these two functions, moreover, is changed one iota by the circumstance that Church government should happen to be the basis for a special civil status.

§ 14. No one person can perfectly possess the full compass of theological knowledge. This is partly because every discipline can be infinitely developed in detail, and partly because the diversity of disciplines requires a variety of talents, all of which one person can scarcely possess to the same degree.

This possibility of an endless development in detail extends to everything that is historical in character, or is somehow connected with historical existence, and to every sort of technical rule covering the variety of situations which might arise.

§ 15. Yet, if everyone should decide, on this account, to confine himself wholly to some one part of theology, the whole of theology would exist neither in one person nor in all together.

Not in all together, for with such a division of labor there would be no way for experts from different fields to cooperate. In fact, strictly speaking, they would not be able to communicate at all.

§ 16. Therefore, if one is to deal with any one of the theological disciplines in a truly theological sense and spirit, he must master the basic features of them all.

Only when each person in a general way comprehends the whole, along with his own special discipline, can each and all communicate. Only thus can each person exert an influence upon the whole through his main field.

§ 17. Whether a man strives to perfect a certain discipline, and which discipline he selects, are matters determined chiefly by the peculiar nature of his own talent, but also partly by his apprehension of the current needs of the Church.

In any given period, the favorable advancement of theology as a whole largely depends upon whether outstanding talents are found to serve the most pressing needs. Those who achieve a certain balance in cultivating the largest number of disciplines, without striving for expertness in any one of them, are always in a better position to exercise the most varied influence. On the other hand, those who devote their attention wholly to one area are in a position to accomplish most in a purely scholarly way.

§ 18. The following factors, then, are indispensable for every theologian: (a) first, an adequate perspective over the ways in which the various parts of theology interrelate, and of the particular value of each for serving the overall aim of theology; (b) then, an understanding of the internal organization of each discipline, and of those principal parts which are most essential for the whole structure; (c) further, an acquaintance with aids for quickly obtaining whatever information may be required; and (d) finally, practice and confidence in applying the necessary precautions for making the best and the most apt use of what others have produced.

The first two points are often covered under the heading of "Theological Encyclopedia"; and the third, i.e., an acquaintance with basic theological literature, is probably to be included within the same scope. The fourth is part of the art of criticism, which has not been worked out as a full-fledged discipline, and for the practice of which only a few rules can be passed on in any case, so that its attainment depends almost entirely upon natural ability and experience.

§ 19. If one desires to master a particular discipline completely, he must make it his aim to sift and supplement what others have contributed to it.

Without such an effort, no matter how complete his information may be, he would be a mere carrier of tradition—the lowest rank of all the activities open to a person, and the least significant.

§ 20. The encyclopedic outline which is to be given here corresponds only to the first requirement noted in § 18, except that it also deals with the individual disciplines in the same manner as with the whole.

Customarily, such an outline has been called a "formal encyclopedia" as opposed to "material encyclopedias," which tend rather to provide a brief sketch of the principal contents of individual disciplines than to give a very exact outline of their organization.

Insofar as it is of the nature of encyclopedia to present an initial introduction to theological studies, there also belong to it certain technical considerations on procedures by which these studies are to be carried on—what is ordinarily called "methodology." The present condition of our academic institutions and of our academic literature, however, presents a problem. For, except for what methodology emerges automatically from such an outline of the internal organization of theological disciplines, it all depends too largely on fortuitous circumstances even to warrant devoting a special section to methodology here.

§ 21. Insofar as one tries to make do with a merely empirical method of interpreting Christianity, he cannot achieve a genuine knowledge of it. One's task is rather to endeavor both to understand the essence of Christianity in contradistinction to other churches and other kinds of faith, and to understand the nature of piety and of religious communities in relation to all the other activities of the human spirit.

That the essence of Christianity is attached to a certain history merely determines more precisely what mode of understanding is required; by itself, however, this fact cannot be supposed to prejudice the task of understanding what Christianity is.

§ 22. Unless religious communities are to be regarded as mere aberrations, it must be possible to show that the existence of such associations is a necessary element for the development of the human spirit.[7]

---

7. In the first edition, ethics was singled out here for this task. In keeping with CF §§ 2-6, it retains this role in the final edition too. See §§ 23-24; 29; 35 below. The *Addresses,*

In recent times, the first attitude has appeared in various views on the nature of Protestantism. Genuine atheism is the tendency to look at piety itself in this way.

§ 23. Any further elaboration of the notion of religious community must also indicate the manner and degree in which one may differ from the others, and likewise how the distinctiveness of the various societies of faith which have arisen in history relates to these differences. Philosophy of religion is the place where such tasks are to be carried out.

To be sure, "philosophy of religion" is not used here in an entirely customary sense, for here it is intended to designate a discipline which, by its reference to the idea of "church," relates to ethics in a similar fashion as another which refers to the idea of "state" and still another which refers to the idea of "art."

§ 24. The part of Christian theology we call philosophical theology utilizes the framework developed in philosophy of religion, in order to present (a) that perspective on the essence of Christianity whereby it can be recognized as a distinctive mode of faith, and at the same time (b) the form which Christian community takes, and (c) the manner in which each of these factors is further subdivided and differentiated. Everything that belongs to these three tasks, taken together, forms the work of philosophical theology.

This use of the term "philosophical theology" is justified partly by the connection of its task with ethics and partly by the constitution of its content, in that a large part of its work is to define concepts. Such a discipline, however, has thus far never been exhibited or recognized as a unit; and the reason is that the need for it, as it is conceived here, first arises only with the problem of organizing the theological sciences. Even so, the subject matter of the discipline has already been worked up fairly completely, as a result of practical exigencies which have developed at various junctures in history.

§ 25. The purpose of leadership in the Christian Church is to hold the various concerns of the Church together and to build on them further, both in a comprehensive as well as in a concentrated way. The knowledge concerning this activity forms a kind of technology which, in combining all its different branches, we designate as practical theology.

---

though written in popular style, in large part represent an application of ethics to the concerns of theology (compare 169n). "Philosophy of religion," in the sense defined in § 23, could be strictly applied only to the fifth address, on "The Religions," but again with the qualification that this is popular not scientific discourse.

Earlier work in this discipline too has been extremely erratic. Administrative details have been copiously discussed. What relates to the work of real leadership and planning, however, has on the whole received but scanty attention, and what systematic work has been done has treated the individual parts of this discipline in isolation from each other.

§ 26. Good leadership of the Church also requires a knowledge of the whole community which is to be led: (a) of its situation at any given time, and (b) of its past, with the realization that this community, regarded as a whole, is a historical entity, and that its present condition can be adequately grasped only when it is viewed as a product of the past. Now these two things taken together constitute historical theology, in the broader sense of the term.

The present simply cannot be regarded as the kernel of a future which is to correspond more nearly to the full conception of the Church, or to any other notion, unless one perceives how it has developed out of the past.

§ 27. Since historical theology attempts to exhibit every point of time in its true relation to the idea of "Christianity," it follows that it is at once not only the foundation of practical theology but also the verification of philosophical theology.

It will be able to fulfill both roles the more easily, of course, the greater the fund of historical developments which lies ready to hand. Thus it can be understood why Church leadership was at first rather a matter of right instinct, and why philosophical theology manifested itself only in fits and starts of little power.

§ 28. Accordingly, historical theology is the actual corpus of theological study, which is connected with science, as such, by means of philosophical theology and with the active Christian life by means of practical theology.

Since a correct understanding of any given period must also demonstrate by what prominent ideas the Church was governed, historical theology also includes the practical aspect in its work; and on account of the connection pointed out in § 27, philosophical theology is also reflected in what historical theology does.

§ 29. If philosophical theology were adequately developed as a discipline, the whole course of theological study could begin with it. For the present, however, its individual components will only be acquired fragmentarily along with the study of historical theology, though even this is possible only when preceded by the study of ethics, which we must regard as being at the same time the science of the principles of history.[8]

Without constant reference to ethical principles, even the study of historical theology is reduced to a kind of haphazard calisthenics, and is bound to degenerate into a process of handing down meaningless information. The lack of such references goes a long way toward explaining the confusing state of theological disciplines which is often encountered and the total lack of trustworthiness in their application to matters of Church leadership.

§ 30. Not only can the technology regarding Church leadership which is still lacking proceed further only through the improvement of historical theology, which in turn requires the agency of philosophical theology, but even the ordinary formulation of rules for administrative duties can only have the effect of a mechanical prescription so long as it is not preceded by the study of historical theology.

Out of a premature occupation with this technology arise a superficiality in practice and an indifference to scientific progress.

§ 31. The whole of theological study is composed of this trilogy: philosophical theology, historical theology, and practical theology. Indisputably, therefore, the most natural order for the present outline is to begin with philosophical theology and to conclude with practical theology.

No matter with what part we might choose to begin, we should always have to presuppose a great deal from the other two, on account of the close interrelation the three have to each other.

---

8. This definition of ethics remains intact from the first edition.

PART ONE

On Philosophical Theology

INTRODUCTION

§ 32. The distinctive nature of Christianity no more allows of its being construed purely scientifically than of its being apprehended in a strictly empirical fashion. Consequently, it admits only of being defined critically (compare § 23), by comparing what is historically given in Christianity with those contrasts by virtue of which various kinds of religious communities can be different from one another.[1]

Although general rubrics can be specified for indicating characteristic differences between individuals, no purely scientific model of a man's true distinctiveness can be constructed. The same is true regarding the distinctiveness of such collective or moral "personalities" as religious communities.

§ 33. The point of departure of philosophical theology, therefore, can only be taken "above" Christianity, in the logical sense of the term, i.e., in the general concept of a religious community or fellowship of faith.[2]

In accordance with what was stated in the foregoing paragraph, every particular mode of faith can be rightly understood only by means of its relations of coexistence and sequence with others. This point of departure would be the same, then, for any analogous disciplines of other

1. On the task of criticism, see §§ 35-37. He returns to this proposition again in §§ 59 and 255-256. See index for "criticism," also for the important contrast between "empirical" and "speculative" (=scientific, in a particular sense).

2. "Above" only "in the logical sense" (as he also notes of a similar passage in § 6 of the first edition of *Der christliche Glaube;* see Martin Redeker's edition, Berlin, 1960, vol. 2, p. 500), for the original controlling factor even in the preliminary definition of Christianity provided through philosophical theology is, for Schleiermacher, God's revelation of himself in Christ, and this is not yet indicated by the "general" concepts used. "There is only one source from which all Christian doctrine is derived, namely, the self-proclamation of Christ; and there is only one type of doctrine, for whether more perfect or less perfect it all arises out of the religious consciousness itself and its direct expression" (CF § 19:P.S.). See § 65.

theologies, in that they must all refer back to the same overall concept and to the possibility of its being subdivided, in order to set forth those relations.

§ 34. The relation of any historically given condition of Christianity to the idea of Christianity itself is determined not alone by the makeup of this condition but also by the manner in which it has come into existence.

To be sure, the two factors imply each other, since it is only possible for conditions differently constituted to have been produced by a different process, and vice versa. It is all the more clear, moreover, that sometimes one of these factors can be used more extensively to discover that relation to the idea of Christianity, and sometimes the other factor. Finally, it is self-evident that not all the various conditions existing within a living, historical whole have the same relation to its idea.

§ 35. It should be made clear that ethics, as the science of the principles of history, can also represent the manner in which a historical whole has come into existence only in a general way. Likewise, it is only critically, by comparing the general differences exposed in ethics with what is historically given, that it is possible to discover what within the development of Christianity is a pure expression of its idea and what, on the contrary, must be regarded as a deviation from it and therefore as a diseased condition.

Diseased conditions do occur in historical entities, no less than in organic. To speak in terms of subordinate differences in development would be off the point here.

§ 36. As long as Christianity is divided into a plurality of Church communities, all of which claim to be "Christian," the same tasks will also arise in respect to these. Thus, besides the general discipline, a special philosophical theology will also be required for each one.

Obviously, this is the situation in which we find ourselves today. Even if every one of these separated communities were to declare all the rest diseased, our point of departure (see § 33) would still demand that our first task be to subject all these claims to critical treatment. Our own special philosophical theology happens to be Protestant.

§ 37. The two tasks of philosophical theology stated here—in § 32 and § 35—exhaust its aim. Thus, two aspects of its work are to be kept in mind: (a) that, in accordance with its scientific contents, it operates as criticism, and (b) that, in accordance with the nature of its object, it operates as historical criticism.

Everything is included in the carrying out of these tasks which is necessary in order to form a basis for the relation of both historical and practical theology to Church leadership.

§ 38. As a theological discipline, the form of philosophical theology must be determined by its relation to Church leadership.

This, of course, also applies to every special philosophical theology.

§ 39. Just as every person is really a part of the Church community to which he belongs only by virtue of his conviction of the truth of the mode of faith propagated there, so also that aspect of Church leadership by which the vitality of the fellowship is maintained must have as its aim to communicate this conviction so that it can be clearly recognized. The foundation for this task is formed by investigations concerning the distinctive nature of Christianity, and likewise of Protestantism; and these constitute the *apologetical* side of philosophical theology. The one set of investigations relates to the general, Christian philosophical theology, and the other to the special philosophical theology of Protestantism.

By this use of the term "apologetics" no other defense is meant than that which seeks to ward off hostility toward the community. The endeavor to bring others into this community is a clerical practice which draws upon apologetics; and a technology for this, which has scarcely begun to be formed, would make up that division of practical theology which rests directly upon apologetics.

§ 40. Since every person, in proportion to the strength and clarity of his conviction, must also experience dissatisfaction over diseased deviations arising in the community to which he belongs, so Church leadership, by virtue of that concentrated aspect of its work by which it maintains a cohesive fellowship (see § 25), must have as its aim to bring such deviations into the light. This can be done only through an authentic representation of the essence of Christianity and, likewise, of Protestantism, which, when applied in this way, forms the *polemical* side of philosophical theology, relating first to its general form and then to its specifically Protestant form.

Principles for clerical activity which is directed toward the removal of diseased conditions are provided here; and the corresponding technology for this would make up that division of practical theology which directly refers back to polemics.

§ 41. Apologetics takes a wholly outward, polemics a wholly inward, direction.

The far more common usage of the term "polemics"—the particular polemics of Protestants directed outwardly, e.g., against the Catholics, or the general polemics of Christians against the Jews or even against deists and atheists—is, again, actually a clerical practice, in the broader sense of the term. On the one hand, this has nothing in common with the polemics we are considering; on the other, it could hardly be recognized as salutary by any practical theology which is well worked out. One might assert, of course, that this practice need not be viewed as specifically Protestant, but only as generally Christian, so that it would be directed inwardly too. But then it would also be directed not against Catholicism as a whole, as it is nevertheless always intended to be, but only against that within it which is alien to its particular form and is thus to be regarded as a diseased condition of Christianity.

§ 42. Since no further tasks remain to philosophical theology than these, the following sections will consider the organization of apologetics and polemics, both in their general, Christian forms and in their special, Protestant forms.

One could either consider general philosophical theology in both its parts, and then, in the same way, the special discipline; or one could first consider apologetics, general and special, and then polemics. The latter arrangement has been preferred.

I. BASIC PRINCIPLES FOR APOLOGETICS

§ 43. Since the concept of religious communities, or of the Church, is realized solely in a body of historical phenomena existing side by side and before and after one another, which possess some unity in that concept but display differences among themselves, it must also be demonstrated, by setting forth both that unity and those differences, that Christianity belongs within this compass. This is accomplished by advancing and employing the correlative concepts of "natural" and "positive."

The advancing of these concepts, the former of which expresses what is common to all, and the latter the possibility of various unique modifications, is actually a task for philosophy of religion. The concepts, therefore, are equally valid for the apologetics of every religious community. Now if philosophy of religion could be appealed to in this way, all that would remain for Christian apologetics would be to fulfill the requirement of the next paragraph.[3]

§ 44. Referring back to the concept of "positive," a formula for the distinctive nature of Christianity must be set forth and then, by showing its relation to the special character of other religious communities, expressed in terms of that concept.

Indeed, this is the basic task of apologetics; but the more it is the case that such a formula can be found only by means of a critical method (see § 32), the more necessary it is for the formula to be fully tested through usage.

§ 45. Christianity must also establish the validity of its claim to a distinct historical existence, by reference to the nature and manner of its origin; and this is done by using the concepts of "revelation," "miracle," and "inspiration."[4]

The more it can be traced back to original facts, the greater is its title to distinctiveness, and vice versa. The same rule also applies to other types of community.

§ 46. However, inasmuch as the historical representation of the idea of the Church is to be regarded as forming a continuous series, so, notwithstanding what was stated in §§ 43 and 44, the historical continuity of Christianity from age to age must also be demonstrated; and this is done by referring to the two concepts of "prophecy" and "type" or "pattern."

Rightly establishing and employing these concepts is perhaps the most important task of this discipline; and the more completely this is carried out, the firmer a foundation is available for the kind of practical application which must build on it further from the outside.

§ 47. Since the Christian Church, like every historical phenomenon, is subject to change, it must also be demonstrated how the unity of its essence is nevertheless not endangered by such modifications as it undergoes. This sort of investigation embraces the concepts "canon" and "sacrament."

---

3. In the CF, this is developed in the "propositions borrowed from the philosophy of religion," §§ 7-10. Compare CF § 11:5.

4. For explication of the terms "positive" and "revealed" see CF § 10:P.S. For "miracle," "inspiration," and "prophecy" see CF §§ 13 and 14:P.S., 75f; also §§ 34:2-3 and 47.

Apologetics does not consider the various dogmatic theories about these two concepts, since such theories cannot be anticipated here.[5] Both facts, however, are conceptually related to the continuity of what is essential in Christianity: canon is so related insofar as this continuity finds expression in the production of ideas, and sacrament is so related insofar as it finds expression in the ongoing tradition of the Christian community.

§ 48. The concept of "church" is admitted into a scientific context only in connection with the common life of all other organizations developing out of the concept of "humanity" (compare § 22). Consequently, it must be demonstrated that, in respect to its particular essence, the Christian Church is able to exist along with all these other organizations; and this must result from a correct analysis of the concepts "hierarchy" and "church authority."

Science and the state especially come into the picture here. For no one could be expected to acknowledge the validity of Christianity if, by its very essence, it should strive against either type of organization, as such. This task, therefore, is the more completely carried out the more definitely it can be shown that, according to the actual meaning of these two institutions within the Church, both aim only at the independent development of the Church in relation to science and the state, and do not intend to disrupt their own equally independent development. Everything regarding this subject which belongs to the work of practical theology is excluded here.

§ 49. In all these investigations, the more regard is shown for two assertions, that Christianity is meant to exist as an organic community and that it is represented and communicated principally by means of thought (compare § 2), the more surely must they lay a foundation for the conviction that, from the very beginning (compare § 44), the essence of Christianity has been rightly apprehended.

If the same essence of Christianity should be found expressing itself in all that relates to doctrine and polity, in accordance with the formula set forth, this would be the best test of the formula.

§ 50. If the Church exists in a state of radical division, then the special apologetics of every distinct party in the Church, and accordingly also

5. The two concepts are not discussed in the CF Introduction, but are implied in § 11. §§ 11-14 there are "borrowed" from apologetics. From the following paragraph, the notion of "humanity" is implied in the propositions borrowed from ethics (§§ 3-6); the others are not discussed.

the apologetics of Protestantism, must pursue the same course as general apologetics.

For the task is the same; and the relation of every party in the Church to the rest resembles the relation of Christianity to other communities of faith akin to it. The matter emphasized in § 47 leads here to the concepts "confession" and "rite"; and in reference to § 48, the most important relation here is that between Church and State.

§ 51. In this case, general Christian apologetics, since it is affected by the viewpoint of every particular formation of Christianity, will also assume a special form in each one.

To be sure, this will be less the case the more strictly everything dogmatic is, as such, excluded from the analysis. Never, however, should the process be carried so far that each party should seek recognition as Christianity only for itself, while regarding all others as unchristian. This should be provided against already by the distinction between general and special apologetics.

§ 52. A plurality of Christian Church communities which stand over against each other can only have been formed out of a condition of the whole, in which no radical contrast had been articulated. Each one, therefore, has to defend itself all the more against the charge of anarchy or corruption, in the degree to which each tends to affirm its own attachment to that original condition.

No radical contrast was articulated in primitive Christianity. Nor can one contrasting form ever appear in the place of another, unless the other has previously disappeared.

§ 53. Since, on this account, every radical contrast of this sort within Christianity seems destined to disappear, the perfection of any special apologetics will consist in the inclusion within itself, in a divinatory manner, of the forms by which this disappearance may take place.

By no means is it intended thereby that a prophetic tendency should be attributed to special apologetics. Rather, the more adequately the distinctive nature of Protestantism is apprehended, in this respect, the more tenable grounds will special apologetics furnish for averting false attempts at union; for every such attempt rests on the assumption that whatever disunity existed has, to some extent, already disappeared.

II. BASIC PRINCIPLES FOR POLEMICS

§ 54. When a historical organism appears diseased (compare § 35), this may be based partly on a recession of vitality, partly on the fact that extraneous factors have entered in and have become organized within it for their own sake.

It is not necessary to refer clear back to the analogy of the animal organism; the same type of situation can also be observed in the diseased conditions of states.

§ 55. Since the impetus to make Christian piety the substance of a community does not necessarily correspond exactly to the actual strength of this piety, sometimes the one can be more weak and recessive, and sometimes the other.

To be sure, the union of both in their fullest perfection composes the normal, healthy condition of the Church, one which can never be presupposed, however, anywhere along the line of its historical career. It is also true, moreover, that this healthy condition can only be described as the complete union of these two factors, and consequently that one-sided deviations are possible on either side.

§ 56. Those conditions under which it is made especially evident that Christian piety itself has become weak and diseased are summed up by the name "indifferentism." Thus, the corresponding task is to determine where such conditions as appear to be weakened actually begin to be diseased, and to indicate the different forms in which each condition presents itself.

This term commonly denotes neutrality with respect to the distinctive character of Christian piety; and it is certainly true that piety may exist without displaying any particular stamp.

It must also be noted that such a weakness is frequently ascribed to conditions which are actually to be explained in an entirely different way.

Naturally, wherever indifferentism is present the impetus to Christian community will necessarily be weakened; but this is to be regarded only as a consequence of the disease, not as its cause.

§ 57. Those conditions which especially indicate a weakening of the impetus to community are designated by the term "separatism," the bounds and structure of which are likewise to be more exactly determined.[6]

6. Compare § 234. Passages on "separatism" in the CF indicate the grounds of his ecumenical position: §§ 87:3,360; 108:5,492; 121:1; 126:1.

A more exact distinction than commonly appears is to be made between separatism proper and an inclination toward schism. This is especially important since separatism, despite its completely negative character, often assumes the appearance of schism. Clearly, whenever the impetus to community is present in its full strength, it must also pervade the whole membership. It is therefore the more weakened the more members there are who consciously and intentionally exclude themselves, despite their claim to possess the same Christian piety.

§ 58. The distinctive nature of Christianity primarily expresses itself in doctrine on the one hand and in polity on the other.[7] Accordingly, an extraneous element can become organized within the Church partly in doctrine, as heresy, and partly in polity, as schism. Thus, the bounds and structure of both of these are also to be determined.

In most cases, though not necessarily all, if a deviation in doctrine becomes widespread a distinct community will also arise from it; but since this is a mere consequence of that condition, it is not to be regarded as an actual schism. Likewise, within a schism, for the most part though not necessarily always, a deviation in doctrine will also develop; but this doctrine need not be regarded as heretical on that account.[8]

§ 59. None of the concepts put forth here can be either discovered by strictly empirical means or derived by purely scientific means. They can be established only by that critical method which is here predominant throughout.[9] Thus, they must be increasingly put to the test through actual use, in order to become wholly reliable.

In respect to schism and heresy, it is necessary, on account of the great diversity of phenomena involved, that this method should rest upon some classification. Such a classification would be validated insofar as the phenomena at hand could be easily included within it. In respect to indifferentism and separatism, the critical method achieves validity in the degree to which it prevents what is still healthy from being declared diseased, through excessive strictness; and vice versa.

§ 60. Of that which is charged of being diseased, it must be demonstrated both (a) that, as to its contents, it contradicts or dissolves the essence of Christianity as this has been expressed in doctrine and polity,

---

7. Compare §§ 49; 60; 90n. For him, the scope of polity is unusually broad (i.e., of *Kirchenverfassung,* not *Kirchenregiment*).

8. On heresy, see CF §§ 21-22. He was extremely wary of making accusations of heresy. See his discussion of "orthodox" and "heterodox" in CF § 25:P.S., 110; and compare §§ 203-211 here.

9. See § 32n.

and (b) that, as to its origin, it does not accord with that mode of development which proceeds from the basic facts of Christianity.

The more these two procedures corroborate and elucidate each other, the more secure the charge.

§ 61. In periods when the Christian Church is divided, the special polemics of any particular Christian Church community has to follow the same path as the general polemics.

The composition of the subject matter is the same, except that in such periods: (a) on the one hand, indifferentism and separatism are, of course, at home, originally in isolated Church communities, and become general evils only insofar as they are similarly met with in several neighboring Christian communities; (b) on the other hand, what only contradicts the distinctive nature of an isolated community, or faction, should never be designated by the expressions "heretical" or "schismatic."

§ 62. The very first beginnings of a heresy always appear as opinions issued by individuals, those of a schism as a banding together of individuals. A new isolated Church community, or faction, cannot very well make its first appearance in any other way. Thus, the basic principles of polemics, when completely developed, should furnish means for readily distinguishing whether such initial elements will result in diseased conditions or whether they contain the germ for development of some new division.

Since this proposition bears practically the same concern as that expressed in § 53, attention should likewise be drawn here: (a) to false tolerance of diseased elements, on the one hand, and (b), on the other, to the responsibility to maintain reasonable freedom for what stands to produce fresh differentiations within the whole.

CONCLUDING REMARKS ON PHILOSOPHICAL THEOLOGY

§ 63. The two disciplines, apologetics and polemics, are both mutually exclusive and interdependent.

They are mutually exclusive because of the contrast in their content (compare §§ 39 and 40) and in their direction (compare § 41). They are interdependent both because what is diseased in the Church can only be recognized by reference to some definite representation of the distinctive nature of Christianity, and because in the investigations upon which this representation is founded the diseased phenomena must also be taken up, provisionally, as part of the basic data to which the critical method is to be applied.

§ 64. The two disciplines, therefore, can attain complete development only by means of and together with each other.

Just on this account, they can do this only by various approximations and transformations on both sides. Compare § 51, since what is said there about apologetics is also true for polemics.

§ 65. Philosophical theology, it is true, presupposes the material of historical theology as already known; its own prior task, however, is to lay a foundation for the properly historical perspective on Christianity.

The material of historical theology is that data which lies at the basis of investigations concerning the distinctive nature of Christianity (see § 32).

§ 66. On the one hand, philosophical theology and practical theology stand together over against historical theology; on the other, they also stand over against one another.

The first assertion is true because those two disciplines are immediately directed toward practical matters while historical theology is directed purely toward observation and reflection. For although apologetics and polemics are, in fact, also theories, from which one may distinguish apologetical and polemical practices, yet these theories only really fulfill their allotted tasks in such practices and would not be set forth except for their sake.

The two also stand over against each other, partly in the relation of first to last, since it is philosophical theology that first fixes the subject matter with which practical theology has to deal, and partly in that philosophical theology fastens upon certain purely scientific constructions while practical theology, in its role as technology, is largely attached to the area of the individual and the particular.

§ 67. Everyone's philosophical theology essentially includes within it the principles of his whole theological way of thinking. Thus, every theologian should produce the entirety of this part of his theology for himself.

This does not mean that any theologian is to be deprived of the possibility of professing adherence to a presentation of philosophical theology which issues from someone else, only that such a presentation must be thoroughly appropriated as one's own firm and clear conviction. It is especially requisite, however, that every theologian should possess philosophical theology fully and completely, irrespective of the provisions regarding general versus specialized knowledge in §§ 14-17; for here virtually everything is fundamental, and the relation of every factor to the rest is extremely close. That all theological principles, moreover, have their place in this sector of the whole theological landscape immediately follows from §§ 65 and 66.

§ 68. Both of the disciplines of philosophical theology still await their mature development.

This fact is already partially understandable in terms of the various circumstances described thus far. On the one side, apologetics has been related too strictly and exclusively to actual apologetical practices, opportunities for which arise only intermittently, whereas the propositions which belong to it have found their place in introductions to Dogmatics —and not without serious detriment to the development of a clear perspective over the whole field of study. Only in very recent times has it even begun to be worked out according to its overall aims and in its true compass. On the other side, polemics long ago ceased to be worked out and handed down as a particular theological discipline, chiefly because its proper direction remained unrecognized.

PART TWO

On Historical Theology

INTRODUCTION

§ 69. Because of its content, historical theology (see § 26) is part of the modern study of history; and thus all the natural divisions of that science are coordinate with it.

Historical theology belongs especially to the inner core of these studies, i.e., to the modern history of ethics and culture, into which Christianity itself has plainly introduced certain developments. For it is clear that the sort of outlook which represents Christianity merely as a source of perversions and retrogressions is out-of-date.

§ 70. Insofar as it forms a theological discipline, the historical knowledge of Christianity is, first and foremost, the indispensable condition of all intelligent effort toward the further cultivation of Christianity; and in this connection all the other parts of historical study are strictly subservient to it.

It is already evident from this what a different turn the study of the same mass of "facts" would take, and even the manner of handling them, when these facts are assigned to historical theology, as compared with placing them within the general study of history. This is true even though the basic principles of historical research do not cease to be the same for both areas of study.

§ 71. Whatever stands out in any given historical area as a moment of particular import can be regarded either as a sudden new beginning or as a gradual development and a further cultivation of something which has gone before.

In the sphere of individual life, every real beginning is sudden and original; but from that point on, everything else is simply a development of what has already begun. However, in the sphere of actual history, i.e., of people's life in common, the two aspects are not so strongly contrasted, and only on account of a preponderance of either is one moment considered in one way and another moment in the other way.

§ 72. The total career of every historical whole consists in various alternations between these two aspects of historical process.

It is not as though it were in and of itself impossible that an entire historical career should be regarded as a continuous development from a single starting point. Still, only two courses are actually open to us: either (a) to look upon the initial force as also containing diverse elements, not all of which become apparent at the same time, or (b) to observe differences of slower and faster progress in the development itself—and one of the two possibilities will scarcely be lacking in any given instance. Consequently, we are already constrained even by this viewpoint to assume that there will always be distinctly contrasting intervals.

§ 73. A series of moments in which a quiet progression of events continually predominates signifies a state of order and forms a historical period. A series of moments in which sudden new beginnings predominate signifies a revolutionary breakdown of previous structures and forms a historical epoch.

The longer the latter, revolutionary situation has continued the more difficult it is to ascertain any identity within the subject matter, since there has ceased to be any clear contrast between the enduring and the changing. Correspondingly, the longer the subject matter has remained one and the same the easier it is to recognize circumstances of the first kind mentioned as predominant.

§ 74. Every historical whole may be considered not only as a unity but also as a composite, each of whose different elements has a career of its own, though only in a subordinate sense and with a constant relation to the other elements.

Such distinction between elements is everywhere present, in some form or other; and there is all the more reason to call special attention to them the more one seems quiescent while another is active and the two thus appear relatively independent of each other.

§ 75. Thus one may follow two modes of procedure for combining the limitless material of a historical career into a clear, overall perspective: either (a) one divides the whole career into several periods, according to the different revolutionary points along the line, and gathers into each period all that has happened in respect to the historical subject being treated, or (b) one divides the subject lengthwise, making several parallel series, and follows each series through the whole of its career.

Of course, the two arrangements may also be combined, so that one is made subordinate to the other. In this way, either each period is divided into parallel series, or each major series is split into periods. The mode of presentation is the more incomplete the more these arrangements are arbitrarily made, or at least the more they are based on superficialities.

§ 76. A historical subject matter requires primarily the first kind of arrangement the less independently from one another its various elements proceed, and consequently the more strikingly the revolutionary nodes in its development rise to prominence. Insofar as the reverse is the case, the other arrangement is preferable.

For in the latter instance, an original structure predominates, and in the former a marked diversity in the character of different ages.

§ 77. The more striking the contrast between periods and epochs in any given historical career the more difficult it is in representing the epochs to separate out the various elements which compose them (see § 74), but the more easy in representing the periods.

For in revolutionary times all interaction is livelier, and every individual element is more dependent upon a common impulse, whereas a quieter situation is more favorable for various distinct elements to stand out.

§ 78. Not only does the total career of all things human, viewed in general, form one whole, but also the entire succession of expressions of one and the same force within it. Thus, whenever a lesser historical whole comes to the fore, it can be regarded in two ways: (a) first as the rise of something new, which was not there before, and then (b) as a development consequent upon something already in some way at hand.

This is already clear from § 71. Although something, in the course of time, may be considered new in comparison with everything that is contemporaneous with it, it may still correspond more exactly to some one earlier moment of history than to all earlier moments.

§ 79. Accordingly, the career of Christianity can also be treated in two ways: (a) as a single period within one branch of religious development, but also (b) as a particular historical whole, which arises as something new and which pursues its own separate course in a series of periods divided by epochs.

Justification for explicitly discussing only one branch of religious development here follows from § 74. However one may classify the great variety of formations of a religious sort, there will always be some so much more nearly related to Christianity than the rest that they can be formed into the same group with it.

§ 80. As a theological discipline, historical theology is entirely related to Christianity, thus it can adopt only the second kind of treatment mentioned above.

Please refer to §§ 69 and 70. The Christian faith, moreover, could not be what it is were not the basic fact of it established, unexceptionably, as something original.

§ 81. If the historical material of Christianity is considered on the basis of the constitutive principle of theology, then the historical knowledge of the present moment of history stands in the most direct relation to Church leadership, since it is that out of which future moments are to be developed. This therefore forms one special division of historical theology.

This discipline would be cultivated so as to be able to exert a right and appropriate influence upon both healthy and diseased conditions, to help any retarded elements move ahead, and to use what is applicable from external or unaccustomed areas for one's own.

§ 82. The present, however, can only be understood as a result of the past, and thus the knowledge of the entire previous career of Christianity forms a second division of historical theology.

This statement is not to be understood as though the second division noted here were a kind of auxiliary science for the first. Rather, both are related to Church leadership in the same way, and are not in a subordinate but are in a coordinate relation to each other.

§ 83. The more any given historical career is occupied in the process of expansion, so that the inner unity of its life appears more and more only in encounter with other forces, all the more do these forces, in turn, enter into the various individual situations which make it up. As a result of this state of affairs, the purest perspective upon its distinctive nature can only come in relation to its earliest expression.

This likewise applies to all kindred phenomena in history, and is the actual reason why so many people mistakenly regard the earliest period of the life of humanity as the age of its greatest perfection.

§ 84. Now since the Christian life has also become increasingly more variegated and complicated, while the final aim of its theology consists in representing its distinctive nature more authentically in every approaching instant of its history, therefore the knowledge of primitive Christianity naturally arises as a third special division of historical theology.

Admittedly, primitive Christianity is also included within the total career of Christianity. It is one thing, however, to treat it as a series of moments, and another only to bring that material into consideration from which the pure conception of Christianity can be represented, even though this may be done with respect to different moments of history.

§ 85. The whole of historical theology is included within these three divisions: the knowledge of primitive Christianity, the knowledge of the total career of Christianity, and the knowledge of the state of Christianity at the present time.

The proper order in which to study them, however, does not correspond to the order in which their derivation has been shown here. On the contrary, the knowledge of primitive Christianity, as most immediately connected with the work of philosophical theology, ought always to be the first stage in one's study, and the knowledge of the present time, as constituting the direct transition to practical theology, ought to be the final stage.

§ 86. For any portion of historical study, any discipline that facilitates acquaintance with the scene of action and with the external relations of the main subject, or that pertains to the understanding of monuments of all sorts, is to be regarded as an auxiliary science. Thus historical theology also draws first upon the other parts of the same historical area (e.g., polemics; see § 40) and then upon all that pertains to the understanding of documents.

Accordingly, such auxiliary studies are partly historical in the narrower sense, partly geographical, and partly philological.

§ 87. With regard to the normal treatment of primitive Christianity already discussed, it cannot be suitably delimited over against the further historical career of Christianity otherwise than by denoting it as that age in which doctrine and community first developed, in their relation to each other, but did not yet exist in their definitive forms.

Yet, even this definition could easily be extended too far, since doctrine and community are continually coming into being, in relation to each other; and a fixed boundary would only be possible to set if one were to exclude every point of time in which a difference in community existed for the sake of a difference in doctrine. But one might also assign limits to the definition which are too narrow, if one were to proceed on the assumption that a distinctive community already existed from Pentecost on. An appropriate extension of the definition will arise only on the premise that the actual Christian community was first definitively constituted when, both intentionally and with general recognition, Jews and Gentiles had become united within it; and the same will also hold in respect to doctrine. Both definitions thus agree fairly well with the more superficial one which assigns primitive Christianity to the generation of Christ's immediate disciples.

§ 88. Since that knowledge of primitive Christianity which is singled out for the purpose indicated can only be obtained from the Christian documents originating within this age of the Christian Church, and rests entirely upon the correct understanding of these writings, therefore this division of historical theology particularly bears the name of exegetical theology.

Since most of what is included in the other two divisions also depends on exegesis, this nomenclature is admittedly arbitrary; its use may easily be justified, nonetheless, on account of the peculiar value of these writings.

§ 89. Every theologian must do his own exegesis for himself, on account of its close connection with philosophical theology, regarded as the locus of all basic principles for theological work; thus, there is very little here, too, that one can allow himself to take over directly from the specialists (see §§ 17 and 19[1]).

For the most part, one would take over only what must be borrowed, for exegetical purposes, from the auxiliary sciences.

§ 90. Knowledge concerning the further career of Christianity may either be set forth as one whole, or be divided into the history of doctrine and the history of community.[2]

Either can be done, since the history of doctrine is simply the development of the religious ideas of the community. The combination of the two, as well as the history of the community presented separately, bears

1. Also see § 67.
2. The word "community" has replaced "polity" from the first edition.

the name "Church history." Similarly, the history of doctrine when presented separately may bear the special name "history of dogma."

§ 91. When viewed lengthwise, both branches, together as well as separately, present an unbroken stream, within which it is nevertheless possible to find certain nodes of development by employing the notions of periods and epochs, in order to fix the distinctions (a) between points along the line which are separated by an epoch and thus belong to different periods, and (b) between those which lie within the same period but in such a way that one rather contains the result of the first while the other appears more as a preparation for the second.

If one should conceive of still further intervening points within a period, which contain the maximum development of its initial epoch but also the starting point of its closing epoch, this process, carried throughout both branches of study, in all periods, would provide a complex of the most valuable moments within the career of Christianity.

§ 92. Since the total career of Christianity presents an endless number of details, there is any amount of room here for the distinction between what is of common concern and what is still a matter for specialists.

The complex of material just mentioned, when drawn together in summary form to present an analogue of continuity within this career, is the minimum which every student of theology ought to possess. The investigation and explanation of details is an inexhaustible task, even when divided among many persons.

§ 93. Not all moments are equally well adapted to representation as a cohesive whole, which mostly belongs to the culminating point of a period, but belongs least of all to any point in or near an epoch.

During a revolution, nothing but details can ever be separated out; and even these can hardly be discussed otherwise than in the form of controversy. It is true that the need for a cohesive representation may already arise in the immediate proximity of an epoch; any attempts at such a time, however, are bound to be incomplete. This situation was manifest both in the early beginnings of the Church during postapostolic times and among ourselves during the early years of the Reformation.

§ 94. In times for which the task can be satisfactorily carried out, the representation of the doctrine of any given community and that of its social condition will separate of themselves.

For even though the same peculiar essence of the Church or of some separate Church community is expressed in both, yet the two depend upon coefficients so different that they must be fairly independent of each other in the changes they undergo, and therefore also in their respective conditions at any given moment.

§ 95. It is the task of Church statistics to represent the social condition of the Church in any given moment.

Only recently has this subject begun to be dealt with in a properly organized manner and within a special discipline.[3] Therefore, much remains to be accomplished, in respect to both content and form.

§ 96. Even when division prevails, the task still remains essentially the same for every individual Church community.

Of course, each community will then have a special interest in being as exactly acquainted as possible with its own situation. Insofar as this obtains, a discrepancy between communities will enter in, which would nevertheless be the case even if the Church were not divided. It can only be greatly detrimental on all sides, however, when the leaders of one Church community are not acquainted with the true condition of the rest.

§ 97. The systematic representation of doctrine which is current at any given time, whether for the Church in general, when division does not prevail, or for any particular party within the Church, we designate by the term "dogmatics" or "dogmatic theology."

The term "doctrine" is taken here in its entire compass. The designation "systematic theology," which is still frequently used to denote this branch of theological study, rightly stresses that doctrine is not to be presented as a mere aggregate of propositions, whose coherent interrelation is not clearly shown. It nevertheless conceals, to the detriment of the subject, not only the historical character of the discipline but also its aim in relation to Church leadership; and numerous misinterpretations are bound to arise as a result.

§ 98. In times when the Church is divided, each party can only deal with its own doctrine dogmatically.

No theologian of one party attempting systematically to compare the doctrine of another party with his own could attain complete impartiality and fairness in his treatment, for only the one organization of doc-

3. Scholz notes: "Schleiermacher is probably thinking of the pioneering work of the Göttingen theologian, C. F. Stäudlin, *Kirchliche Geographie und Statistik,* 2 Teile (Tübingen, 1804)." Schleiermacher had also lectured a full academic year on the subject, in 1826-1827.

trine would bear the truth for him, the other not. This would be the case even if he should deal with his own doctrine systematically, by itself, and then merely adjoin the divergencies of the other in the appropriate places, because these would then be torn out of their own natural connection with each other. The first practice does have its place, however, concerning the main points of doctrine; and it is called "symbolics."[4] The second practice may be called "comparative dogmatics."

§ 99. Both statistics and dogmatics are endless in extent; both bear the same distinction, within this second division of historical theology, between what is of common concern and what is still a matter for specialists.[5]

This is obviously true of Church statistics. It is equally true of dogmatics, however, where finer determinations of each particular doctrine can go on almost indefinitely and where the representation of each doctrine with respect to divergent modes of conceiving them in other times and places is also virtually endless.

§ 100. Each student of theology must form his own historical perspective for himself, concerning both the knowledge of the total career of Christianity and that of the moment of history in which he lives.

Otherwise he will not be able to exercise his own discretion in matters of Church leadership which rest equally on both.

§ 101. Since one is forced to use historical studies for this purpose, studies which can never be wholly divested of the scholar's own particular viewpoints and opinions, every student must possess the art of separating out the material to be used for his own work in the purest state possible.

This applies also to dogmatics and statistics, no less than to Church history.

§ 102. Historical criticism is the all-pervasive and indispensable organ for the work of historical theology, as for the entire field of historical studies.

As a special skill for the "reconciling" of data, its work is quite distinctively different from the production of raw material by the auxiliary sciences.

---

4. See § 249n.
5. Compare § 92.

I. EXEGETICAL THEOLOGY

§ 103. The Christian writings which come to us from the age of primitive Christianity are not the proper subject matter of exegetical theology simply on this account, but only insofar as they are held capable of contributing to the original, and therefore for all times normative, representation of Christianity (compare § 83).

It is of the nature of the case, and is also completely established as a matter of fact, that at the beginning there likewise existed an imperfect, and thus partially false, apprehension—and, as a result, also a partially false representation—of the authentic Christian faith.

§ 104. The collection of those writings which contain the normative representation of Christianity forms the New Testament canon of the Christian Church.

Thus, the correct understanding of this canon is the unique, essential task of exegetical theology; and the collection itself is its unique and original subject matter.

§ 105. Within this New Testament canon belong essentially both those normative documents which concern the action and effect of Christ both on and with his disciples, and also those which concern the common action and effect of his disciples toward the establishment of Christianity.

This was already the intention in the ancient practice of dividing the canon into *evangellion* and *apostolos*. There is no inherent reason for stipulating any difference in canonical value between these two constituent parts. Yet this would be somewhat the case if one should assert that the two do have the relation of origin to further cultivation, and still more so if one were able to deny normative value to the action and effect of the disciples when left to themselves.

§ 106. Neither the temporal boundary of primitive Christianity nor its cast of characters can be exactly determined; consequently the outside boundary of the canon cannot be determined with complete exactitude either.

Admittedly, if both time and persons were taken together, it would be possible to set forth a definite formula of canonicity. This formula, however, still would not lead to any secure decision concerning the material, on account of the uncertainty which prevails regarding the person of several particular authors.

§ 107. This lack of certitude corresponds to a wavering of the boundary between two areas: the writings of the apostolic fathers and the canonical writings.

For the age of the apostolic fathers lies between that in which the canon first came into being and that in which it already possessed a separate existence. Furthermore, the expression "apostolic fathers" is to be understood here as having such scope that the lack of certitude mentioned applies as much to the first part of the canon as to the second.

§ 108. Since the concept of normative value is also one which cannot be reduced to fixed, immutable formulas, it is not even possible to circumscribe the canon by basing such a determination on internal grounds.

If we figure that the normative character of particular propositions includes perfect purity on the one hand, and on the other the fullness of inferences and applications which may develop from them, we have no reason to suppose that the first attribute will exist, absolutely, anywhere but in Christ alone, and must concede that, as to the second attribute, natural imperfection could operate obstructively in all others but not in him.[1]

§ 109. Those Christian writings from the time of the canon to which we deny normative value we designate by the term "apocrypha"; but the boundary of the canon is not completely fixed over against these writings either.

Most of the New Testament apocrypha, of course, bear this name simply because they either claimed or were commonly supposed to belong to the time of the canon. When used in this sense, the term is arbitrary; it would be better to exchange it for some other.

§ 110. The Protestant Church necessarily claims to be continually occupied in determining the canon more exactly; and this is the greatest exegetical-theological task for higher criticism.

The New Testament canon has obtained its present form through the decision of the Church, though this decision cannot be found expressed in any one particular act or declared with exactness. This is not a decision to which we attribute an authority exalted above all inquiry, and thus we are quite justified in starting fresh investigations in connection with earlier waverings of the boundary. This is the greatest task for higher criticism because it is more important to determine whether a piece of writing is canonical or not than to determine whether it is to be

1. See CF §§ 93-94, 98.

assigned to this or that author, in which case it could still be canonical no matter what decision is made.

§ 111. Textual criticism has two kinds of investigation to undertake: (a) concerning whether certain material found within the canon is not, strictly taken, uncanonical, and (b) concerning whether there might be some canonical material outside the canon not yet recognized as such.

Investigations of the second kind have been in process again quite recently; those of the first kind never cease.

§ 112. Both tasks apply not only to whole books but also to particular sections and passages within them.

An uncanonical book may contain new canonical passages, just as most of what has been interpolated by a later hand within a canonical book will be uncanonical.

§ 113. Higher criticism carries out its task, for the most part, only by approximation; and there is no other measure of the soundness of its decisions than the congruence of internal and external evidence. Thus, what is in question here is simply this: (a) how definitely do external signs indicate that a questionable piece of literature belongs either to the times of the apostolic fathers, later on, or to the area of apocryphal treatment, which is remote from the center of the Church, and (b) how definitely do internal signs indicate that it is not apprehended and thought out in exact agreement with what is essential in the canonical representation?

So long as both kinds of evidence conflict, or some signs stand on one side and some on the other of each kind, no critical decision will be possible.

That by "the center of the Church" neither any given realm nor any official post is to be understood here, but only the fullness of Christian sensitivity and insight, doubtless needs no further explanation.

§ 114. If criticism should separate out both types of literature, and arrive with complete security at a new and different definition of what is canonical and what is not, it would still not be necessary to order the canon itself differently on that account.

It would not be necessary because the uncanonical material may still be recognized as such even though it should retain its old position; and the same would be true for whatever is proved to be canonical, even though it should remain outside the canon. It must be permissible then, however, to have the canon in two forms: that which has been handed down historically and that which has been separated out critically.

§ 115. The same applies to the ordering of the books of the Old Testament in our Bible.

That the Jewish codex does not contain any normative statements[2] of peculiarly Christian doctrines will doubtless be recognized almost universally. There is no need on this account, however—although it must remain permissible—to deviate from the ancient Church's practice of uniting the Old Testament with the New Testament into one whole, the Bible.

§ 116. The multiple reproduction of New Testament books on the basis of the originals was necessarily subject to the same difficulties as are encountered with all other ancient writings.[3]

Visual evidence has long ago shattered all the prejudices which formerly ruled concerning this.

§ 117. Not even the huge amount and variety of copies we possess of most of these books provides security against the possibility that the original reading has nevertheless been lost for some passages.

For this loss may have occurred very early, even in the first transcript, and even in such a way that it could not be made good again.

§ 118. The definitive task of lower criticism, everywhere to separate out the original reading as accurately and convincingly as possible, is wholly the same within the area of exegetical theology as it is elsewhere.

The terms "lower criticism" and "higher criticism" are employed here according to established usage, without any intention either of justifying their appropriateness or of defining the boundaries between them more exactly.

§ 119. Accordingly, the New Testament critic has both the duty to follow the same rules and the right to employ the same means as apply elsewhere.

Thus it cannot be forbidden to venture conjectures, where the case demands it (see § 117); nor can there be any special rules which absolutely cannot be derived from rules which apply generally.

2. *Glaubensätze,* from *doctrina fidei*—doctrines directly pertaining to the Christian faith. First edition: "To include the Jewish codex within the canon means to view Christianity as a development of Judaism and contradicts the whole idea of the canon." See CF § 132, and §§ 128-130 and 141 here.

3. This paragraph begins the section on "lower criticism." See his 1830 address "Ueber Begriff und Eintheilung der philologischen Kritik," SW III.3, 387-403.

§ 120. To the degree in which criticism carries out its task, there must also result an exact and comprehensive history of the New Testament text, and vice versa, so that each of these processes may serve to test and support the other.

Even what may be rightly accomplished through conjecture must be able to appeal to evidence appearing in the history of the text; and vice versa, any striking emendations offered must also exemplify the history of the text.

§ 121. As to the theological aim behind being occupied with the canon, the restoration of the original is of direct value only where the normative contents are somehow involved.

In no way is this statement to be limited to so-called dogmatic passages; it is also to be extended to all that can be employed in any way as parallels to or elucidations of such passages.[4]

§ 122. Since the critical task is endless, the previous statement leads to the necessity of making a distinction here between what is to be required of every theologian and what constitutes the area of special studies.

Actually this requirement is only relevant to the Protestant theologian; for, strictly speaking, the Roman Catholic has the right to demand that the Vulgate be delivered to him with not one critical problem remaining.

§ 123. Any theologian—even in the broader sense of the word—may get into a situation where he needs to be convinced on a critical matter (see § 121) for expository purposes (see § 89). Thus each one, in order to appropriate the work of specialists on his own and to choose between their results, must possess not only the basic critical principles and rules relevant to such situations but also a general knowledge of the most important critical sources and of their value.

A meager guide may be found partly in the prolegomena to critical editions of the New Testament, and partly among those various considerations usually referred to as New Testament introduction.[5]

§ 124. All is to be required of every specialist in New Testament criticism that pertains both to a complete, consistent reconstruction of the

4. On "proof" from Scripture see CF § 27:3, also CF §§ 128 and 131:2. Compare §§ 209-210 here.

5. SW I.8 contains his lectures on New Testament Introduction, which he taught only twice, in 1829 and in 1831-1832.

text, which follows the same basic principles throughout, and to a correct and suitable arrangement of the critical apparatus.

These are purely philological tasks. It is not easily supposed, however, that a philologist should turn his skill to such tasks within the New Testament, apart from any interest in Christianity, since this book rates far behind other writings in linguistic importance.[6] If theology should ever lack such specialists, however, there would also be no more security as to what must be done to achieve the theological aim behind this study.

§ 125. Behind all the preceding statements (§§ 116-124) has lain the presupposition that real exegesis, including exposition, can only be done by the person who works with the canon in its original language.

Otherwise the critical task would be of value only for the translator, and even this only within the bounds described in § 121.

§ 126. Since not even the most masterful translation can transcend the irrationality of languages, no discourse or writing can be fully understood except in its original language.

By irrationality is meant simply the well-known fact that neither a material nor a formal element of one language is wholly transferable into that of another language. Therefore, a discourse of writing which is mediated through a translation, and consequently the translation itself as well, can be fully understood only by the person who knows how to trace it back to the original language.

§ 127. The original language of the New Testament books is Greek; but much important material (in accordance with § 121) is to be regarded as a direct translation from Aramaic or as having been indirectly influenced by Aramaic.

Earlier assertions that certain individual books of the New Testament were originally written in Aramaic hardly warrant attention now. Much, however, of what has been preserved in discourses or conversations was originally spoken in Aramaic. Indirect influence is contained in that modification of the language which is known as Hebraism.

§ 128. The numerous references, direct and indirect, to Old Testament writings in books of the New Testament themselves make a closer acquaintance with these writings, and also, therefore, with their original language, necessary.

This is all the more true because these references relate, in part, to some very important passages, in relation to which one's exegesis and ex-

6. This point is repeated in § 147.

position of the New Testament passages themselves must be formed, and consequently a correct judgment as to the relation which the vernacular Greek translation of the Old Testament bears to the original language is indispensable.

§ 129. The more limited the spread and productivity of a dialect, the less fully understandable it is except in connection with all that are akin to it. This fact, when applied to the Hebrew language, demands that for the fullest understanding of the canon there should be an adequate knowledge of all the Semitic dialects as well.

This is why the Arabic and Rabbinical dialects have been drawn into Biblical interpretation all along.

§ 130. This requirement, however, which includes a great deal that is quite foreign to the immediate aim of our theological studies, is to be placed only upon those who desire to master exegetical theology, and even then only in this particular direction.

The same is true for this purely philological direction within such studies as was stated in § 124.

§ 131. In the area of language proficiency, it is to be expected that every theologian will attain (a) a basic knowledge of Greek, especially of the various developments of Greek prose, (b) a knowledge of both the original languages of the Old Testament and, by this means, a clear insight into the nature and compass of Hebraism in the New Testament, and (c) finally, in order to make use of the work of specialists, not only an acquaintance with the literature of the entire field but especially an independently formed judgment regarding what is excessive and insufficient, natural and artificial, in the employment of oriental material.

For errors are constantly being committed in this area, out of partiality on the one hand and prejudice on the other.

§ 132. The full understanding of a discourse or piece of writing is a kind of artistic achievement, and thus requires an "art doctrine," or technology,[7] which we designate by the term "hermeneutics."[8]

We apply the term "art," in an even narrower sense, to every ordered production whereby we are conscious of certain general rules whose application to particulars cannot be reduced to still other rules. The common practice of restricting hermeneutics to larger works or to difficult

7. Compare § 265.

8. "Dogmatics can only reach its consummation simultaneously with the theory of Scriptural exegesis" (CF 27:3,116). Compare §§ 209-210, 219 here.

details is without justification. Rules can form a technology only when they are derived from the nature of the entire procedure and consequently also comprehend the entire procedure.

§ 133. Such a technology exists only insofar as its rules of interpretation form a system resting upon principles directly evident from the nature of thought and language.

So long as hermeneutics is handled as a mere aggregate of isolated observations, whether general or particular, it will not yet deserve the name of technology, no matter how fine and noteworthy these observations may be.

§ 134. Protestant theology cannot accept any representation of the canon which would exclude the use of this technology from its proper business.

For this latter would be possible only if one should somehow assume a miraculously inspired and perfect understanding of the canon.

§ 135. The New Testament writings are especially difficult to interpret, both on account of their inner contents and on account of their external relations.

The first point is true because the communication of particularly unique religious ideas, in their early development, by writers largely from a less cultured sphere, who were handling in an irregular fashion a language not their own vernacular, can very easily be misunderstood. The second is true because the various circumstances and relations which modify the course of thought are largely unknown to us and can first be surmised only from the writings themselves.

§ 136. By virtue of the particular aim of exegetical theology, the New Testament canon is to be handled as one whole, while each individual writing regarded in and of itself is nevertheless a separate whole. Insofar as this is the case, there is adjoined a special task of balancing and combining these two modes of treatment.[9]

The complete exclusion of one or the other of these standpoints, resulting as it has from opposing theological extremes, has in all ages introduced error and confusion into the business of interpretation.

§ 137. The special hermeneutics of the New Testament can consist only of more precise determinations of the general rules of hermeneutics,

9. First edition: "The goal of all interpretation consists in rightly apprehending each individual thought also, at the same time, in its relation to the idea of the whole, and so to reconstruct the act of writing. . . ."

made however with reference to the particular situation of the canon.

It is all the more important that the development of New Testament hermeneutics toward the stricter form of a technology should be gradual, since it was founded at a time when even general hermeneutics still existed only as a collection of observations.

§ 138. The technology of interpretation can be formed in two ways. In either setting, however, it constitutes the proper center of exegetical theology.

That is: either (a) general hermeneutics comes very much to the fore, so that the special hermeneutics appears only as a corollary; or (b) the special hermeneutics may be systematically organized in such a way that it need only refer back to general principles.

It is certainly true that hermeneutical practice is conditioned by linguistics and criticism;[10] hermeneutical principles themselves, however, exert a most decisive influence both upon the operations of criticism and upon the finer observations of linguistics.

§ 139. Thus, here too there is nothing which would allow one to rely on others. Each person must rather strive to attain as great a mastery as possible.

The more completely the subject has been worked out, the less should this mastery seek to display itself in new interpretations.

§ 140. No writing can be fully understood except in connection with the total range of ideas out of which it has come into being and through a knowledge of the various relations important to the writers' lives and to the lives of those for whom they write.

For every writing bears a relation to the collective life of which it is a part, just as a single sentence relates to the whole discourse or writing in which it appears.

§ 141. Thus, the historical apparatus for explaining the New Testament writings includes a knowledge of earlier and later Judaism and of the cultural and civil condition of those regions in which and for which these writings were composed.

Accordingly, the Old Testament books are the most general aid for understanding the New Testament; next in importance are the Old and New Testament apocrypha, the later Jewish writers as a whole, and the historians and geographers of that time and place. All these aids like-

10. That is, criticism in the restricted sense employed in §§ 110-124. In another sense, hermeneutical practice is also criticism—historical criticism (see index).

wise require use in their original languages, critically and according to the rules of hermeneutics.

§ 142. Up to the present time, many of these aids have not been used as fully as they might be, or with proper caution.

Both assertions are especially true regarding contemporary and later Jewish writings.

§ 143. This whole apparatus, then, will claim the activity of many theologians for a long time to come, in order to correct and supplement the previous work of specialists in this field.

From another perspective, such previous work reverts to apologetics, in recognition of the fact that opponents of Christianity have continually attempted to explain it solely on the basis of what was already given, and indeed not always as an advance and improvement. What is involved here, however, is simply the pure and complete preparation of the historical material.

§ 144. What is suitable for common consumption among all this material will be imparted partly under the heading of Jewish and Christian Antiquities, and partly in conjunction with various other matters in what is called Introduction to the New Testament.

In the latter, which no doubt needs a general reworking, one still misses much material that nevertheless especially belongs to it, according to § 141, since one should bring the material to his reading of the New Testament.

What each person may allow himself to take from the work of specialists in this field is found partly in compilations from various sources and partly in commentaries on individual books of the New Testament.

§ 145. Thus far, the major task of exegetical theology is in no way to be regarded as completely executed.

This is true even when one discounts the fact that there are particular passages some of which will never be emended with complete surety and others of which will never be explained to the satisfaction of all.

§ 146. A twofold task also persists regarding the auxiliary information which relates to exegetical theology: (a) to work toward the completion of this material, and (b) to convert whatever is ready into common property.

The first study, carried out under the direction of specialists, must not only lay the foundation for the second and on this basis begin application in accordance with the rules of technology. It must also at least open up the different individual areas with respect to that mastery of the subject which is yet to be attained.

§ 147. Any extended occupation with the New Testament canon which is not motivated by a genuine interest in Christianity can only be directed against the canon.

For the purely philological and historical gain of which the canon gives promise is not rich enough to attract a person to such an occupation.[11] Still, even the investigations of opponents (see § 143) have been very useful, and will continue to be so in future.

§ 148. Every occupation with the canon which lacks philological intelligence and skill must remain within the bounds of general edification, for in the theological field it could only produce confusion by its pseudo-dogmatic tendency.

For such a procedure cannot be founded on a pure and firm desire to understand.

II. CHURCH HISTORY

(*Historical Theology in the Narrower Sense*)

§ 149. Church history in the broader sense (see § 90) is knowledge concerning the total development of Christianity since its establishment as a historical phenomenon.

The effect of Christianity externally, apart from that development, does not belong in this field of study.

§ 150. Every historical mass may be viewed (a) on the one hand as one indivisible being and doing in process of becoming, and (b) on the other hand as a compound of innumerable individual moments. Genuinely historical observation consists in the combination of both.

(a) The first is simply the characteristic spirit of the whole viewed as to its mobility, and without a distinct separation of facts. (b) The other is simply the enumeration of its diverse states, but without their being conjoined according to their identity of impulse. Historical observation consists in both ways of viewing: (a) the concentration of a congeries of facts into a single picture of their inner reality,[1] and (b) the representation of this inner reality in the separating out of these facts.

---

11. Compare § 124.

1. "Reality" is added in translation; *das Innere* can be used to refer to the inner self, heart, or soul of a person, hence here the inner being and doing, idea or spirit, of a historical mass.

§ 151. Accordingly, every fact has historical individuality only insofar as the two are posited as identical: the outer reality as the changing of what nevertheless maintains its identity, and the inner reality as the function of a force in motion.[2]

In this manner of speaking, the "inner" is posited as soul, the "outer" as body—the whole, consequently, as a life.

§ 152. The perception and retention in memory of spacial changes is almost a sheer mechanical operation, whereas the construction of a fact, the combination of outer and inner into one historical perspective, is to be regarded as a free action of the mind.[3]

Thus, even though several persons may perceive something as entirely the same they will still apprehend it as a fact differently.

§ 153. The depiction of spacial changes as such, in their contemporaneousness and succession, is not history but chronicle; nor would such a depiction of the Christian Church be able to validate itself as a theological discipline.

For it would not supply those factors within the total career of Christianity which have a relation to Church leadership.

§ 154. Events which are not to be regarded as actual historical elements must also be admitted into a historical account, but only for the sake of continuity.

These include changes within persons who were active in distinguished positions, even though their personal characteristics did not exercise any marked influence upon their public behavior.

§ 155. Apprehending things historically is a talent, one which is developed in each person, though in varying degrees, through the resources of his own historical life but which can never entirely dispense with mechanical skills.

Within the area of science, as in ordinary life, an aroused self-interest and consequently anything of a factious sort distorts one's historical view more than anything else.

---

2. Newtonian physics has its obvious influence upon this typical use of the term "force" (compare § 160). His sense of the integral relation of inner and outer factors in any historical reality, however, implies rejection of any purely mechanistic interpretation of human events.

3. "Talent" was the term used in the first edition; compare § 155. The term *geistig* is hereafter (§§ 312-334) translated in the broader, more literal sense of "spiritual," though intellectual activity is ordinarily the focus of meaning.

§ 156. Historical knowledge of what is not personally experienced may be obtained in two ways: (a) directly through the use of primary sources, though with the attendant difficulty of getting a full picture, and (b), more easily, though only indirectly, through the use of historical presentations.

It would scarcely be possible to do without the latter in any field of history, certainly not in that of Church history.

§ 157. Sources in the narrower sense we call "monuments" and "documents," which witness to a fact in that they themselves make up a part of it.

In this stricter sense, even historical descriptions by eye witness are not to be regarded as sources. Yet, the more they approximate chronicle, and simply repeat quite unpretentiously what was observed, the more they deserve the name, too.

§ 158. In using the historical presentations of others, one can arrive at a historical account of one's own only insofar as one eliminates what has been interpolated by the author in each case.

This is made easier if one can compare several portrayals of the same series of facts, all the more so if these are taken from different points of view.

§ 159. One attains to such knowledge of a total situation as depicts its inner reality (see § 150) only by combining a mass of details which belong together into their proper relations.

This is thus the greatest contribution a person's gift of historical apprehension can produce, one which both presupposes and involves everything else.

§ 160. As a theological discipline, Church history in the broader sense (see § 90) ought above all to distinguish between what has resulted from the distinctive force of Christianity[4] and what is founded partly in the make-up of the various organs thus set in motion and partly in the influence of principles foreign to them, and then to try to gauge the advance and recession of each.

However, the plan of dividing the delineation itself on this basis into favorable versus unfavorable events has produced a very faulty method.

4. See §151n. According to usage of the time, every force or principle has its own distinctive "functions," i.e., aspects of movement by which its own particular action is carried out and can be identified. This is assumed in the following paragraphs.

§ 161. From the outset of Christianity, and therefore already in the time of primitive Christianity, one can distinguish and also separate from each other within one's historical delineation various functions of this new effective principle. These functions are themselves capable of being subdivided much further.

This is also generally true of all important historical phenomena, including all religious and civil communities.

§ 162. The development of none of these functions, however, can ever be fully understood apart from its relation to the others; and every division of time which can be separated out as a relative whole becomes what it is only through the correlative influence of these functions upon each other.

For the vital force of Christianity is wholly posited in every given moment of its history, and can therefore be grasped only with respect to the mutual conditioning of all the different functions.[5]

§ 163. The total career of Christianity can be completely apprehended, therefore, only by variously combining both kinds of procedure, since each is needed to supplement at one point what the other has failed to provide at another.

As long as we are tracing out only one function, our eyes lack perspective over the total life of Christianity, and we must resolve eventually to retrieve this. As long as we are working to bring many contemporaneous factors into one focus, we are not in a position to estimate individual elements accurately, and we must resolve to compare them eventually with similar elements which precede or follow.

§ 164. In historical observation, the more one splits up the different functions into minute details the more often must one insert points in between which will reunite what has been disjoined. The larger the parallel masses being considered, the longer may one continue to observe their individual elements without such interruption.

The periods, therefore, may be larger if the functions dealt with are larger in scope; they must be smaller if the functions are smaller.[6]

---

5. This is a different point from that in §§ 83-84. Here he is leading up to his discussion on two basic functions: doctrine and life. The first edition read: "Since the Church is a community of doctrine as well as of life, neither of these two functions [*Functionen*] is to be understood as to its activity apart from the other, and each aspect [*Moment*] can only be vitally and correctly apprehended by being regarded in its inseparable relation to the other."

6. On periods and epochs, see §§ 73-79, 91-93, 199-200.

§ 165. The most important points within an epoch,[7] however, are those which not only have a similar value for all the functions of Christianity but are also significant for historical development outside the Church.[8]

Since the appearance of Christianity is in itself a turning point in world history, other phenomena approach it in importance only insofar as they resemble it in this respect.

§ 166. The cultivation of doctrine, or the process by which the religious self-consciousness gains clarity, and the forming of common life, or of the impetus to community as it is satisfied in each person through all and in all through each person: these are the two functions within the development of Christianity which are most easily separated.[9]

This is recognizable in the fact that great changes may occur on the one side while everything remains as it was on the other, and that a given point in time may be significant as a node of development for the one side but appear to be unimportant for the other.

§ 167. From without, the cultivation of the Church's life is determined[10] above all (see § 160) by political circumstances and by the whole condition of society, whereas the development of doctrine is determined by the whole state of science and especially by prevailing philosophical views.

This accompanying determination is natural and unavoidable. Consequently, it does not in and of itself entail the existence of diseased conditions, though it certainly does contain the ground of their possibility.

More general epoch-making points which emerge from a new development in knowledge will be manifest for the most part in the history of doctrine, whereas those which emerge from developments in civil affairs will be manifest for the most part in the overall communal life of the Church.

§ 168. On the side of the Church's life, the two functions most easily separated are the development of common worship, i.e., of the manner in which the religious elements in life[11] are publicly communicated, and

---

7. On points within an epoch see also §§ 93, 171-172, 186.

8. This external relation is most evidently revealed in the Church's polity. See § 175.

9. On "religious self-consciousness" see CF §§ 3-6 and 17, Addr. II. In Schleiermacher's view, community is of the essence of religion; see also Addr. IV.

10. The term is *mitbestimmt,* thus determined from with-out, as it were; and so the phrase "from without" is added in translation. The inner determinants are of a different, but not totally different, kind.

11. In § 166, *fromme* is the term translated "religion." Here the phrase *religiöse Lebensmomente* especially refers to those elements in human life which have a more

the development of morality, i.e., of the common impression which the influence of the Christian principle makes upon the various areas of action.

Common worship relates to morality in the same fashion as the more limited area of "art" in the narrower sense[12] relates to the less specifically defined area of social life in general.[13]

§ 169. From without, the development of common worship is determined[14] above all by the character of those means of expression suited to it and available in society, and by the way these means are distributed within society, whereas the further cultivation of Christian morality is determined by the general development and distribution of cultural resources.

Regarding the first point, any actual communication or circulation of religious stirrings which is to correspond to their nature will thus rest solely upon the manner in which they are re-expressed. Regarding the second point, any motives for action of which the religious disposition is to take possession will thus rest in the general cultural situation mentioned.

§ 170. Both morality and worship, however, are also so closely conjoined in their ongoing cultivation that when they diverge too much from each other, in either movement or repose, then either common worship comes to look as though it has degenerated into empty ceremonies and superstitions while the Christian life is clearly demonstrated in morality, or, vice versa, Christian piety is maintained through common worship while prevailing morality appears merely to convey the consequences of motives foreign to Christianity.

These diverse critiques manifest an inner antagonism among members of the Christian community, which corresponds to the divergence of worship and morality from each other.

§ 171. The more suddenly any important changes enter into either of

---

noticeably religious character than others. He does not mean that religion is a completely separate part of our life, or that it pertains more to what we do inside than outside a service of worship.

12. For explanation of this use of "art" as technique see §§ 132, 265; for the relation of such art to worship see § 280.

13. See his liturgical writings in SW I.5 and his lectures on practical theology in SW I.13.

14. See § 167n. First edition: "Morality indicates how the religious disposition enters into the various aspects of human action and how it relates to all other sources of motivation."

these two areas the more numerous the reactions to which they will be exposed. In contrast, only slower transformations prove to be thoroughgoing.

The first assertion is self-evident only regarding changes which do not encompass several areas at once. It is only too easy, therefore, to regard such changes as epoch-making events prematurely, especially in view of the fact that they often leave few traces behind them.

§ 172. Slow transformations cannot be apprehended as a continuous series, but can only be brought into perspective at certain prominent points which exhibit the progress made from one time to another.

These points, moreover, must not be selected arbitrarily, but must bear a resemblance, even if only in a subordinate sense, to points which are clearly epoch-making.

§ 173. In this area, historical apprehension is the more complete the more definitely the relation of the Christian impulse to the moral and technical constitution of society is in view and the more convincingly whatever belongs to the healthy development of its religious principle is divorced from what is weak and diseased.

For it is in this way that the need for Church leadership of a Christian account of history is satisfied.

§ 174. The Church's polity—especially in the evangelical Church, where it is not subject to any external sanction—can only be considered as belonging to the area of morality.[15]

This proposition, rightly understood, lies beyond the pale of all those controversies over evangelical Church law which still prevail. It simply expresses the essential difference between civil and ecclesiastical government.

§ 175. Those greater nodes of development which affect civil life as well as the Church will be revealed within the Church most directly and unmistakably in its polity.

This holds true simply because no other part of Christian morality is so closely connected with political circumstances (see § 167).

§ 176. The history of the Christian life as a whole is most fittingly represented when it follows that sequence which is exhibited in the development of the Church's polity.

15. See his addresses on polity in SW I.5. On this relation, also see §§ 269, 318-319.

For polity exerts the most direct influence upon common worship, is indebted to the general condition of morality for its support, and likewise expresses the relation between the religious and the civil communities.

§ 177. Doctrine is developed on the one hand through continual reflection upon Christian self-consciousness in its various aspects, and on the other hand through the continual effort to fasten down its expression more precisely and with more general agreement.[16]

Each of the two processes is a check on the other, in that the first has an inward and the second an outward direction. From this it is seen how different periods can be characterized by the preponderance of one process or the other.

§ 178. Accordingly, the order in which the various points of doctrine arise and in which the main constellations of didactic language are formulated must be capable of being directly conceived, on the large scale at least, from the distinctive nature of Christianity.

For it would be unnatural if notions which most nearly relate to the distinctive nature of Christianity should be developed last of all.

§ 179. Only in a diseased condition of the Church can the personal suasion of individuals or, for that matter, even pressures from outside the Church exert any significant influence upon the course and results of doctrinal study.[17]

Though such circumstances have admittedly been the case, and not infrequently, recent historians in particular have still attributed far more influence to them than is conformable to the truth.

§ 180. The less the development of doctrine can remain free of fluctuation and discord, the more prominent becomes the effort partly to demonstrate the agreement of any given statement with the utterances of primitive Christianity and partly to refer to propositions granted elsewhere which are not engendered by Christian faith as such and which are thus to be regarded as philosophical propositions.

Both attempts would be made, though doubtless not without some

---

16. First edition: "The gradual formation of doctrine is, on the one hand, the progressive reflection upon the Christian principle in all its relations, and on the other, the search for those places within the current system of philosophy which may aid in expressing Christian feeling." See §§ 180-181 for the place of philosophy in the second process.

17. First edition: "Completely external circumstances cannot constitute the true basis for important decisions in the area of doctrine."

delay and not to the same degree, even if there were no dominant controversy. For the communal spirit[18] of Christianity already presses toward the former, and toward the latter presses the need to be convinced of the agreement between religious self-consciousness as it gains clarity and what is being produced through speculation.

§ 181. Only within a diseased condition can these two attempts become so opposed that one party refuses to employ anything beyond the utterances of primitive Christianity toward the definition of doctrine, while another party introduces philosophical propositions into Christian doctrine without desiring to demonstrate that they also pertain to Christian consciousness by reference to the canon.

The former retards the development of doctrine, just as the latter obscures and falsifies its principle.

§ 182. Knowing the changes which the relation between the two tendencies sustains is essential to an understanding of the development of doctrine.

Only too often, by neglecting such factors, one produces mere chronicle instead of history, and the theological aim of the discipline is thus entirely lost.

§ 183. It is equally important to take cognizance of the relation between movements in the area of theoretical doctrine and those in the area of practical dogma.[19] Where these movements widely diverge, it is natural to separate the history of dogma proper from the history of Christian ethics.

To be sure, there have been on the whole more diverse and energetic movements within the formation of doctrine proper (*Glaubenslehre*) than within that of ethics (*Sittenlehre*). It is all the more important, then, not to overlook the opposing tendency.

§ 184. If we bear in mind how much auxiliary knowledge is required in order to follow out these various branches of Church history, it is patent that this area is endless and that it postulates a broad distinction between what every student of theology ought to possess and what is furnished only by the united efforts of specialists (see § 92).

---

18. *Gemeingeist* is always primarily a theological category for Schleiermacher, referring to the action of the Holy Spirit, not to an independent group spirit. See CF §§ 123, also 110:2, 507; 116:3, 535; 121:2; 122:1, 565; 122:3, 568f; 127:1; 129:1-2, 595; 130:2, 598; 132:2, 609; 133:1; 141:1, 652; 144:1, 661. In contrast, a consensus or common disposition would be a *Gemeinsinn* (as in § 313 below).

19. See § 223.

Insofar as everything is to be understood in the fullness of its relations,[20] the entire science of history as it is relevant to any given time belongs to this auxiliary knowledge. Insofar as everything is to be derived from the sources, the entire study of philology wherever relevant, and especially documentary criticism, also belongs.

§ 185. In general it can only be said that out of this boundless compass each student of theology must possess whatever contributes to his own responsible participation in the leadership of the Church.

This formula may appear rather narrow. It presupposes, however, that in addition to his particular and local activity each person will also strive to exercise a general influence, even though its effects may not be distinctly demonstrable.

§ 186. Now, since at any given time the state of affairs out of which a new moment of history is to be developed can only be grasped in relation to the entire past, although the most recent epoch-making situation is still the most pertinent to it,[21] therefore an adequate perspective over the latter situation is the first major requisite, as clarified by an understanding of its relations to all the principal revolutions which have preceded it.

Obviously, particular notice to the possibility that the present moment is actually more of a preparation for a future epoch is out of the question here; for this can only first be judged when a relation to that epoch already exists in history.

§ 187. However, lest such an account should remain a series of isolated, disconnected pictures, its material must be conjoined through that complex (see § 91), rather fully displayed, of the primary moments from each branch of Church history within each period.

Since this is the foundation for any activity a person might do on his own, the survey must also be constructed, wherever possible, from different kinds of accounts.

§ 188. But even this account will develop into a vital historical perspective, one which contains a forceful impulse of its own, only when the total career of Christianity is apprehended at the same time (see § 150)

---

20. The phrase *im Zusammenhang,* here translated "in the fullness of its relations," is of key importance, referring to his sense of the integral relation of all human knowledge and experience.

21. First edition (now § 212 in revised form): "The most recent epoch in the history of Christianity is the Reformation, through which the opposition between Protestant and Catholic has been established." See CF § 23.

as the depiction of the Christian spirit on the move, and when everything is consequently related to one inner reality.[22]

Only when it has taken this form can knowledge of the total career of Christianity affect Church leadership as it should.

§ 189. Every local exercise of influence calls for a more exact knowledge of that particular area, one which is the more complete the more nearly it relates to the present.

The rule is automatically modified according to the extent of the locality, since it is often the case that the smallest locality, that of a single congregation, has no special history but can only claim attention as part of a larger whole.[23]

§ 190. Each person should also practice some personal research and use of sources, on at least one small part of history.

This should be done, whether one only refers carefully and consistently to the sources in this study, or whether one attempts to construct something on his own from them. Otherwise one could hardly have even so much historical-critical technique at one's command as would be requisite for a right use of divergent accounts.

§ 191. A study of Church history which goes beyond this point must have the intention of contributing something new.

Nothing is more fruitless than a piling up of historical learning which neither serves any practical purpose nor offers anything for the use of others in its presentation.

§ 192. These fresh studies may aim not only at correcting or completing the material, but also at a greater truth and vitality in its treatment.

The deficiencies which persist in all these respects are unmistakable, and are easily accounted for.

§ 193. Ecclesial and scientific interest must not be allowed to fall into contradiction with each other in the study of Church history.

Since we have resolved to lay down no rules for others, we limit this proposition to our own Church. Insofar as it is an inquiring and self-

22. See §§ 180n on "spirit" and 150n on "inner reality." First edition: "The overall spirit and character of an age can only be fixed within the scope of a great historical *(historischen)* picture. Who cannot sketch such a picture for every age does not live in history *(Geschichte)*."

23. Compare § 277 below; and see Addr. 196-198, where he tries to put the problem of larger and smaller Christian communities in ecumenical perspective.

cultivating community, even the most complete impartiality cannot be supposed to do it any harm, but only to serve to its benefit. Therefore, not even the liveliest interest of the evangelical theologian in his Church should necessarily prejudice either his research or his account of it. And just as little is it to be feared that the results of his research will weaken his ecclesial interest—in the worst instance they can only give him the impetus to cooperate toward the removal of known deficiencies.

§ 194. Anyone's work on Church history must partly emerge from his own inclination and partly be determined by the opportunities which present themselves to him.

A lively interest in theology will always enable one to know how to turn the former toward the latter, or even to procure the latter for the sake of the former.

III. HISTORICAL KNOWLEDGE OF THE PRESENT CONDITION OF CHRISTIANITY
[*Dogmatic Theology and Church Statistics*]

§ 195. Here we have to do with dogmatic theology (see §§ 94-97), as the knowledge of doctrine now current in the evangelical Church,[1] and with Church statistics, as the knowledge of the existing social condition in all the different parts of the Christian Church.

The place here assigned to dogmatic theology—which, also under the name of "systematic theology," has occupied quite a different position in other schemes—must be justified through the exposition to follow. At this juncture it is only to be pointed out that the two disciplines named exhaust the above heading, in its entire compass. This is clarified by the fact that since the Church is wholly to be regarded as a community, there is actually nothing in it which would not be recognized as part of its social condition. Doctrine is only taken up separately because its delineation lends itself to special treatment, and needs it. Of course, this could also be done with other aspects of its social condition, but these have not been worked out as theological disciplines thus far. If, however, in times when the Church is divided, it is only possible for each larger community within the Church to work out its own doctrine in the form of dogmatics (see § 98), this raises a problem. How is the evangelical theologian to come to know the doctrine current in other communities of the Christian Church? And what place can our Outline assign for this purpose? The most direct approach would be through the dogmatic accounts which they themselves give of such doctrine, which would, how-

1. First edition: "That theological discipline which is known under the name of thetic or dogmatic theology has to do with the systematic presentation of doctrine now current in the Church." Compare the slightly different wording in CF § 19, taken over without change from the first edition of the CF in 1821.

ever, become mere historical reports for the evangelical theologian. The place preferred for this in our Outline is in the history of Christian doctrine traced down to the present moment, for which those accounts are the genuine sources. But statistics too may include a special place for doctrine in dealing with each community.

A. Dogmatic Theology

§ 196. A dogmatic treatment of doctrine is not possible without personal conviction, nor is it necessary that all treatments which relate to the same period of the same Church community should agree among themselves.

One might wish to draw both statements from the fact that the dogmatic treatment only has to do with the doctrine current at a given time (see §§ 97 and 98). Only this would not suffice, for the person who is not convinced of this doctrine, though he might well provide a report on it, and even on the manner in which the ordered structure of the doctrine is conceived, cannot establish the truth of this structure through the disposition he makes of it. Yet it is only this latter factor which makes the treatment dogmatic. The other is merely a historical treatment of the sort which a person who knew enough could give similarly of all systems.

Full agreement, moreover, is not necessary in the evangelical Church, since even at the same time different views may have currency for us, side by side. Thus, everything is to be regarded as having currency which is officially affirmed and officially heard without arousing strict official opposition.[2] Of course, the boundaries of differentiation are thus more broadly or narrowly set according to time and circumstances.

§ 197. The statement and support of a body of propositions which are preponderately deviant and which express merely the conviction of an individual we would not term a "Dogmatics"; nor would we use the word for any such presentation which is offered in a time marked by a divergence of views but which would only admit what is uncontroversial.

No one would deny the first restriction. Yet, one controversial question deriving from it still serves to confirm our notion, namely the question as to whether textbooks on doctrine are really presenting dogmatics when they merely give a historical report on current doctrine and only offer support for propositions which might have official objections leveled against them.

Regarding the second restriction, a purely irenical compilation of doctrines would end up so meager and indefinite that the middle terms

2. On "currency" see CF § 19. The term is *geltend,* which bears the meaning of valid more than of prevalent; "currency" has been chosen because it is neutral and its meaning can be more easily supplied in context. See also CF §§ 27:P.S., 117; 39:3; 64:1, 265.

necessary to form a demonstrative argument would be generally lacking, as would the precision in defining concepts necessary for winning confidence in the presentation.

§ 198. Dogmatic theology serves the leadership of the Church, to begin with, by showing in how many ways and up to what point the principle of the present period has developed itself on all sides, and how the germs of improved formulations still to come relate to this principle. At the same time, it gives practical activity the norm for popular communication, so as to guard against the recurrence of old difficulties and confusions and to prevent the introduction of new ones.

This latter, practical interest falls entirely within the conservative function of Church leadership, and it was from this that the gradual cultivation of dogmatics originally proceeded. The two parts of the first statement are explained by what was said earlier, in a more general context, about the contents of each moment in history (see § 91).

§ 199. In every historical moment which can be represented separately (see § 93), that within its doctrine which flows out of the preceding epoch comes forth as having been most determined by the Church; but that which rather opens the way for a future course appears as due to the work of individuals.

The former element is not only more markedly determined by the Church than the latter, but also than what has simply been taken over from earlier periods. The latter element is all the more to be traced back only to individuals the less definitely a new formulation of doctrine can be anticipated.

§ 200. All points of doctrine which are developed through the dominant principle of the period must agree among themselves, whereas all others, so long as one can only say of them that they do not have this point of departure, appear as separate points without unity or interconnection.

The dominant principle itself, however, may be variously apprehended, and this may give rise to several dogmatic presentations, coherent in themselves though differing from each other, all of which lay claim—and perhaps not without reason—to a like degree of ecclesiality.[3]

When the single, heterogeneous elements are consolidated, either they present themselves as a new apprehension of the principle already dominant or they announce the development of a new one.

3. Compare § 215.

§ 201. A complete knowledge of the present state of doctrine embraces not only what is essentially implicated in its ongoing cultivation but also what may not have been insignificant as a personal view but, as such, will nevertheless eventually fall out of the mainstream. Consequently, a comprehensive dogmatic treatment must take into consideration everything relevant to its own Church community at the time.

A place for this will always be found if comparisons and parallels are not neglected in the effort to support the organization of doctrine set forth.

§ 202. A dogmatic presentation is the more complete as it possesses a divinatory as well as an assertory character.

In the assertory character of the presentation is shown the degree of surety in one's own view; in its divinatory character is shown the degree of clarity with which one apprehends the whole existing state of doctrine.[4]

§ 203. Every element of doctrine which is construed in the intention of holding fast to what is already generally acknowledged, along with any inferences which may naturally follow, is "orthodox." Every element construed in the inclination to keep doctrine mobile and to make room for still other modes of apprehension is "heterodox."

It seems too narrow to apply these terms exclusively to the relation which doctrinal opinions bear to some particular norm, for the same contrast can also be found where there is no such norm. In accordance with the above explanation, it is much more possible for a creedal symbol to originate from the orthodox direction, and so it has happened often enough. What may appear strange in this explanation, however, is that it does not refer at all to the content of propositions in and of themselves, and yet this is also easily justified on closer observation.

§ 204. The two elements are equally important, both in respect to the historical course of Christianity in general and in respect to every significant moment as such within its history.

No matter what uniformity of doctrine might exist, there would still be no true unity without the orthodox element. Likewise, no matter how great the diversity of doctrine, there would still be no conscious and free mobility without the heterodox element.

§ 205. It is false orthodoxy to wish to retain in dogmatic treatment

4. Compare CF § 16.

what is already entirely antiquated in the public pronouncements of the Church and does not exercise in its scientific expression any definite influence upon other points of doctrine.

Inquiry into such a determination of doctrine would obviously have to be set in motion again, and carried back to the point where this originated.

§ 206. It is false heterodoxy in dogmatic treatment to inveigh against formulations which have well grounded support in pronouncements of the Church and the scientific expression of which does not create confusion regarding their relation to other points of Christian doctrine.

This is not meant in any way to justify that servile, accommodating spirit which would leave standing anything that happens to be used by many people for edification, even though it should not be possible to reconcile it with the basic doctrines of our faith.

§ 207. A dogmatic presentation intended for the evangelical Church will avoid both these aberrations and, despite that mobility of the letter which we have affirmed, will still be able to be orthodox in all the major points of doctrine. Yet, despite the aim of confining itself to what has currency, it must also bring heterodox material into the process.

If this discipline is consistently developed from its proper notion, the natural relation between the two elements will always be what is set forth here, and will be forced to change only when one of the two extremes has been predominant for a long time.

§ 208. Every dogmatic theologian who either innovates or exalts what is old, in a one-sided manner, is only a very imperfect organ of the Church. From a falsely heterodox standpoint, he will declare even the most impeccable orthodoxy to be false; and from a falsely orthodox standpoint, he will combat even the most mild and inevitable heterodoxy as a destructive innovation.

It is these extreme oscillations which have hitherto been principally to blame for the fact that the dogmatic theology of the evangelical Church has almost continually been prevented from advancing peacefully.

§ 209. For every doctrinal proposition taken into the organization of dogmatics the manner in which it is determined must be verified, partly by referring its contents directly or indirectly to the New Testament canon and partly by showing that its scientific expression agrees with the composition of kindred propositions.

All propositions which are referred to in this latter sense, however, are subject to the same rule. Hence there is no other subordination here than this: that those propositions least need either of these operations whose popular, scriptural, and scientific expression are most nearly identical, so that every fellow believer may verify them at once by the certainty of his own immediate religious self-consciousness.[5]

This distinction will probably survive that between fundamental and nonfundamental articles, which, as it is commonly understood, is already to be regarded as out of date.

§ 210. If the treatment of the canon is significantly altered, the procedure for verifying doctrinal propositions must also be altered, even if their content should remain the same.

The orthodox interest within dogmatic theology ought never to stand in the way of exegetical investigation or to dominate it; but the omission of special, so-called proof texts is, in and of itself, no testimony against the correctness of a valid doctrinal proposition. On the other hand, canonical support whose validity is sustained will necessarily grant security to a doctrinal proposition against the heterodox tendency.

§ 211. In regard to the propositions which definitely express the distinctive character of the present period, tracing them back to the creedal symbol may replace canonical verification, provided we are still able to appropriate the interpretation which had currency then.[6]

In such cases it will also be advisable to stress agreement with the creedal symbol, in order to distinguish these propositions more definitely from others (see §§ 199, 200, 203). This, however, in no way applies to propositions which have been transferred by sheer repetition from earlier periods into the symbol of the present period.

§ 212. The distinctive character of evangelical Church doctrine is inseparable from that opposition between the evangelical and the Roman Churches first fixed as an outcome of the Reformation; consequently any proposition traced back to our symbols is only to be regarded as completely elaborated insofar as it bears opposition within itself to the corresponding propositions held by the Roman Church.

---

5. See § 121n on proof, and § 166n on religious self-consciousness.

6. See CF 27:1-2 and Addr. 193f, 206f. His 1819 address on symbolic books, a preface to preaching on the Augsburg Confession, and his letters of 1831 to von Cölln and Schulz on the subject are included in SW I.5; the noted series of sermons on the Augsburg Confession, also from 1831, are in SW I.2.

For it would not be possible to find sufficient verification, by reference to the symbol, for a proposition in relation to which the opposition had already been abrogated on our part, or for one to which this opposition was foreign.

§ 213. The strictly didactic form of expression, which, by contributing toward the interconnectedness between individual doctrinal formulations, gives the dogmatic procedure its scientific frame, is dependent at any given time upon the existing condition of the philosophical disciplines.[7]

This is partly on account of the logical relation of these formulations to each other, and partly because many definitions of concepts refer to psychological and ethical elements.

§ 214. The dialectic element in doctrine may join onto any philosophical system that does not exclude or deny the religious element by its assertions, either in general or in that special form of it to which Christianity professes immediate adherence.

Therefore, regarding all decidedly materialistic and sensualistic systems, which, however, one could indeed hardly let pass as genuinely philosophical (and all genuinely atheistic systems will also have this character), none of them is to be employed in doing dogmatics. For general purposes, it is difficult to set limits any narrower than these.

§ 215. Individual doctrines may therefore be differently conceived in dogmatic treatments produced at the same time, and may also read differently at different times, while in both cases no difference presents itself in their religious contents.[8]

This is so on account of the difference between coexisting or successive schools and their terminologies. It is only through misunderstanding, however, that dogmatic controversies arise over such differences.

§ 216. In the same manner, propositions may appear similar whose religious contents are nevertheless more or less different.

It is not only differences in detail between various theological schools of the same Church which can be concealed behind the identity of sci-

---

7. For further explanation of "didactic" and, in the next paragraph, "dialectic" see CF §§ 16 and 28. His controversial lectures on the attainment and organization of knowledge are entitled *Dialektik* (SW III.4:2). Material on didactic and other forms of religious language is also to be found in his lectures on *Pädagogik* (SW III.9) and *Praktische Theologie* (SW I.13, especially 201-320).

8. See § 200, also §§ 206, 219.

entific terminology. Protestant and Catholic propositions can also appear equivalent, especially when they are somewhat remote from the main points of the creedal symbols.

§ 217. The Protestant treatment of dogmatics must strive to bring clearly into consciousness the relation of each point of doctrine to the predominant opposing contrast of our period.

This is a need in Church leadership which can be satisfied only in this way; for in Church leadership an incorrect notion of the present state of this opposition—concerning whether and where it is already disappearing through a drawing near of the two parties, or whether and where it is just beginning to develop itself more definitely—necessarily gives rise to great difficulties and confusions.

§ 218. In its total compass, dogmatic theology is endless, and this requires a distinction between the area largely reserved for specialists and that which is common property.

This distinction, of course, relates only to the extent of the material to be worked on, not to the security and strength of conviction, nor to the manner in which these are attained.

§ 219. It is to be required of every evangelical student of theology that he be engaged in forming a personal conviction regarding every proper locus of doctrine: not only as these have been developed from the principles of the Reformation as such, and in opposition to Roman doctrines, but also insofar as anything new has taken shape whose historical significance, at least for the present moment, is not to be overlooked.

By a "locus" I mean any proposition, or group of propositions, which has a definite place within the canon and the creedal symbol but also cannot be passed over without causing others of the same compass and value to become obscure and unintelligible.

The expression "be engaged in forming a personal conviction" in no way implies a skeptical frame of mind, but rather that inward receptivity to new investigations essential to the spirit of our Church: either to changes in the treatment of the canon, or to the opening up of new sources for dogmatic terminology. This requirement, moreover, does not relate directly to that faith which is the common possession of all Christians, but to the strictly didactic composition of statements about this faith.

§ 220. The study of dogmatics must therefore begin with the apprehension and testing of one or more well-connected delineations of what is established in the Church, as a further development of the symbols, which are by their very nature only fragmentary.

An accompanying knowledge of the history of dogma will necessarily be presupposed, if only in such features as the nonspecialist is able to master.

For the rest, one should distinguish between, and respectively group together, those delineations which develop their propositions predominantly from the letter of the symbols and those which profess to remain faithful to the spirit of the symbols while subjecting their letter to criticism.

§ 221. In regard to new material which is not explicable in terms of the symbol, it must first of all be decided upon reflection, insofar as such material belongs to this area of study, whether some of this points back to a common origin and betrays a common design.

For the more this is the case the more safely it can be supposed that such views have a historical footing.

§ 222. Accurate knowledge of all contemporary modes of treatment, of all unsettled controversial questions, and of all careless opinions, and a firm judgment as to the ground and value of these formulations and elements together constitute the area of speciality in dogmatics.

This "firm judgment" is to be understood with the qualification of that fresh receptivity (see § 218) which is no less necessary to the master than to the beginner.

By "careless opinions" are to be understood not just the ephemeral phenomena derived from a whimsical and disordered person, but also all that which, as actually diseased, is to be reduced to anti-Christian or at least to anti-evangelical impulses, and thus becomes a subject for the practice of polemics.

§ 223. In earlier parts of this Outline, little notice has been taken of the division of dogmatic theology, which now prevails, into treatment of the theoretical side of doctrine, or dogmatics in the narrower sense, and the treatment of its practical side, or Christian ethics—all the less so because this separation cannot be regarded as essential; for neither in the evangelical Church nor in general is this something belonging to the basic origins of the discipline.

Neither the designations "theoretical" and "practical" nor the terms "faith-doctrine" (*Glaubenslehre*) and ethics, or "moral doctrine" (*Sit-*

tenlehre), are fully adequate.[9] For rules for the Christian life are also theoretical propositions, as developments of the Christian concept of the good; and they are also faith-propositions, statements of faith, no less than those which are dogmatic proper, since they too have to do with the same Christian religious self-consciousness, only in its particular manifestation as motivation.

Now, it cannot be denied that the treatment of the two together belongs to a period in the history of theological studies which was in many respects incomplete. Nevertheless, it is also true that a progressive improvement of this area of study may well be conceived apart from such a separation.

§ 224. This separation does afford to both sorts of proposition the advantage of being more easily apprehended in their respective interconnections. It has brought to Christian ethics the further advantage of undergoing a more elaborate treatment.

This latter advantage, however, is not essentially a consequence of the separation. For a treatment in which the two are conjoined is also conceivable, one in which the relationship was just the reverse of what actually existed before the tendency to separate them arose; and then the separation would have led to the same advantage on the side of dogmatics. Over against the first advantage mentioned, a well-ordered, vital conjunction of the two would appear to provide special security against the ease with which dogmatic propositions proper can degenerate into lifeless formulas and ethical propositions into bare, external prescriptions.

§ 225. The division of this area of study can very easily give rise to the assumption that among entirely different interpretations of faith-doctrine there could still be the same interpretation of ethics, and vice versa.

This error has already penetrated very deeply into the common life of our Church. It can be effectively countered only by doing dogmatics scientifically.

§ 226. This division finds considerable justification both in the fact that support from the canon and the creedal symbol is formed in a significantly different way for ethical propositions than for dogmatic propositions, and in the fact that their respective terminologies stem from different areas of science.

In this relation, it is true that we have referred the theological sciences in general to ethics and the disciplines dependent upon it. If we consider dogmatic theology in particular, however, we find that the

9. See § 183.

terminology of faith-doctrine proper rests largely upon that philosophical science which used to have its place in metaphysics under the name of "rational theology,"[10] whereas Christian ethics can draw for the most part only from discussions about duty in philosophical ethics.[11]

§ 227. Separation of the two disciplines has also generated an inverted, eclectic procedure, under the illusion that one may proceed without ill effects to refer to a different philosophical school for Christian ethics than for faith-doctrine.

One need only picture to oneself the possibility of an undivided treatment of dogmatic theology to find this procedure absolutely inadmissible.

§ 228. This separate treatment is the more appropriate the less uniform the course of the period has actually been between the two disciplines, in relation to the development of its principle[12] and in relation to the tension between the two great opposing positions,[13] or, at any rate, the less evenness there has been in scientific observation of the actual course of events.

One would perhaps be wrong to assert that the contrast between Protestantism and Catholicism is less developed in regard to morality than in regard to faith; but it seems undeniable that in our Christian ethics this opposition is not nearly so fully worked out as in our dogmatics.

§ 229. Undeniably, there are many elaborations of Christian ethics in which only a faint glimmer of the proper type of theological discipline appears, and which are only slightly distinguishable from philosophical ethics.

That this necessarily exerts a most damaging influence upon Church leadership is clear. In an undivided treatment such a result could not take place for ethical propositions unless faith-doctrine were also to deny its own character.

§ 230. The separate treatment of these two branches of dogmatic theology will be the less objectionable the more completely all that was

---

10. Compare § 1.
11. Compare § 223. Most of the numerous writings on philosophical ethics are collected in two large volumes of *Schleiermachers Werke,* edited by Otto Braun (Leipzig, 1928), including special critiques on the concept of "duty."
12. Compare § 198.
13. See §§ 212, 217.

said in §§ 196-216 is also applied to Christian ethics, and the more the interconnection of the two disciplines is reinstated by means of cross-references.

The first suggestion cannot be elaborated here in detail. The possibility of the latter is evident from what was said in § 224.

§ 231. It will always remain desirable that the undivided treatment should regain currency from time to time.

Without going into very great detail such a treatment would scarcely be possible; only it should be done in such a way that the mass of material does not lose all form.

B. Church Statistics

§ 232. Within the overall social condition of a Church we distinguish between its internal constitution and its external relations; and in the first we further distinguish between whatever contents admit of being indicated and the form in which that Church exists as a society.[14]

To be sure, it seems that many particulars can be as easily included under the one head as under the other; but yet such would always be in a different relation in the two instances, so that this does not detract from the correctness of our classification.

§ 233. In times when the Christian Church is not outwardly united, this task embraces all the several Church communities.

Each is then to be considered in itself, and the relations of each to the rest naturally find their place in a second half of the discipline.

But even if the various Church communities were not definitely separated from each other, particular sections of the Church would still differ so much from other sections, both in their inner constitution and in their outer relations, that classifications would still have to be made.

§ 234. The contents of a Church community at any given time are based on the strength and uniformity with which the common spirit[15] characteristic of the community pervades the entire mass of people belonging to it.

Above all, therefore, its contents are on the whole based on its state of health as regards indifferentism and separatism (see §§ 56 and 57). This

---

14. First edition: "Knowledge of the present situation of the Church, or Church statistics, especially concerns the religious development, polity, and external relations of the Church throughout Christendom." On internal-external relations see § 150n.

15. See § 180n.

will be recognized, on the one hand, from various exponents in the development of doctrine, with a view to the unanimity or multiplicity of the results and to the particular interest of the community in this or that function. On the other hand, it will be recognized from the influence of its characteristic group spirit upon the other areas of life, and especially from its manifestation within the worshiping life of the people.

§ 235. The greater the difference in contents existing within widely extended Church communities the less to the purpose of this discipline it is to be contented with accounts giving mere averages.

What is most instructive for Church leadership would be lost if no comparison were made of the most dissimilar factors with regard to the most important points which come under consideration.

§ 236. The nature of the form under which a Church community exists, i.e., of the form of its polity, rests upon the manner in which the leadership of the Church is organized and upon the relation of the entire body to those who participate in Church leadership, i.e., to the "clergy" in the broader sense.

The great diversity of polities makes it necessary to divide them into certain major groupings. However, care should be taken thereby that one does not lay too much stress upon their analogy with political forms, and that one does not overlook their specific differences in deference to their general character.

§ 237. Depicting the internal constitution of a Church is the more complete the more it offers means for rightly estimating the influence of its polity upon its internal condition, and vice versa.

For this joins upon the greatest task of Church leadership; and without such a comparison all accounts belonging here remain dead notices, as do all statistical figures apart from an intelligent combination of findings.

§ 238. The external relations of a Church community, which can only be relations to other communities, are partly relations to similar communities, namely those of Christianity and of particular Christian communities with non-Christian communities as well as those of Christian Church communities to each other; and they are partly relations to communities of a different kind, notably to civil society and to science[16] in the fullest sense of the term.

16. See §§ 48, 167.

We consider the latter a community if only for this reason: that language conditions all scientific communication, and that each language moreover forms a special communal area, so that the relations of the same Church community may be altogether different in different language-areas.[17]

§ 239. Every Church community stands in a relation of communication as well as of reaction toward other communities with which it is in contact. This can be quite variously graded, from a maximum of the one with a minimum of the other to the opposite extreme.

By "contact" is to be understood not just local contiguity but intercourse of any kind. Reaction, moreover, even apart from all outwardly directed polemics, is partly conditioned by the fact that a common reference is made to the canon and partly by progressive activity originating from without, which can never be regarded as wholly lacking.

§ 240. The relation of Church communities to particular bodies of knowledge fluctuates between two extremes. The one extreme occurs when the Church will not accept any knowledge except what it can adapt to its own aims, consequently any knowledge it cannot bring forth on its own. The other extreme occurs when objective consciousness claims for itself truth which is attainable only by self-consciousness.[18]

For the two kinds of community exclude each other at both these points. Midway between the two extremes, there lies, as a point of mutual approach, an active recognition of each by the other. The task here is to bring light to bear on the relationship of such communities to these main points on the continuum.

§ 241. The same is true for the relation between Church and State, except that in this case, in which more definite forms of relation develop, one more readily sees that it is not easy for mutual recognition to take place without the weight's falling slightly to the one side or the other, and also that evangelical Christianity in particular assigns definite limits to its claims.

That a theory regarding this relation does not belong here needs no explanation. Many of the topics indicated here, however, are also treated in what is called "Church law" (*Kirchenrecht*), only predominately viewed, as the name itself implies, from the standpoint of civil life.

17. "Language" is obviously not restricted to French, German, etc., here, but refers to different language usages bound up with different interests displayed in the effort to obtain knowledge, i.e., different "scientific" interests. See CF § 15.

18. These are two different kinds of consciousness, though inseparable. "Self-consciousness" refers to that kind of awareness which comes, more subjectively and immediately, out of oneself—in this case out of the inner experience of the Church. See § 295n.

§ 242. As these main features show, Church statistics can be carried out endlessly.

Naturally the discipline must be continually refurbished, since more accrues to the contemporary elements of Church history whenever changes occur.

§ 243. Among us, students of theology only too often restrict their knowledge to the condition of the evangelical Church, even to that part of it within which their own activity lies. Such a restriction has a highly injurious effect upon the practice of the Church.

Nothing so much favors persistence in the customary and traditional as the ignorance of strange and yet kindred circumstances. And nothing brings on a more uncouth fanaticism than the fear of having to recognize elsewhere something good which is lacking in one's own circle.

§ 244. A general knowledge of the condition of Christendom as a whole, in all the major circumstances specified here and according to the measure in which each part is associated with the circle of one's own activity, is an indispensable requirement for every evangelical student of theology.

The obligation to obtain an accurate knowledge of what is nearer and more closely related, which certainly follows from the above statement, is still only subordinate. For a proper influence upon one's own Church community is only possible when one works within it as within an organic part of the whole, a part which has to maintain and develop itself vis-à-vis the other parts.

§ 245. Much remains to be done by devoting special attention to this field of study, concerning both matter and form.

Recently much material has been produced, it is true; but seldom has it been taken hold of from the right point of view. And there are still so few works of a more comprehensive sort that the best form cannot possibly have been found as yet.

§ 246. The mere external description of what is given is in the same relation to this discipline as chronicle is to history.

In the present state of the discipline, however, it is still profitable to bring things unknown and out-of-the-way into the general fund of knowledge. Merely topographical and onomastic or bibliographical notices are, of course, the least fruitful among such kinds of information.

§ 247. A detailed inquiry into the present condition of Christianity which does not proceed from ecclesial interest or assume any relation to

Church leadership could produce only an uncritical collection of information, especially if it is also pursued in a nonscientific spirit. The more scientific its character, however, the more skeptical or polemical it would tend to become.

On account of the nature of the subject, the impetus cannot originate from a purely scientific interest. Therefore if an interest in the matter itself is lacking, then an opposing interest must be operative. The situation is similar in the case of Church history.

§ 248. If a person's religious interest is bereft of a scientific spirit, this inquiry will not yield a true result, but will simply serve the subjectivity of the person or of his party.

For where a powerful interest prevails, which originates in self-consciousness, only the scientific spirit can afford security against uncritical partiality.

§ 249. The discipline which is normally called symbolics is simply put together out of elements belonging to Church statistics and can be completely broken down again into these elements.[19]

It is a compilation of what is distinctive in the doctrine of various Christian parties still existing; and since this cannot be put together after the manner of dogmatics (see §§ 196 and 233), with verification of the whole organization of doctrine, the presentation must be purely historical (*historisch*).[20] The name "symbolics" does not entirely correspond to the subject matter, since not all parties have symbols in the ordinary sense of the word. Thus, it can only be intended to mean that the rèport given holds to the most classical and the most generally acknowledged representation of each mode of faith. Within statistics (see § 234), such a report must form the basis for exhibiting the role of doctrine within the community; and so the difference is merely that in statistics the doctrine of a community is described in conjunction with the other circumstances of that community, while in symbolics it is described in conjunction with the doctrine of other communities—although we have already recommended (see § 235) that the comparative method be adopted for statistics as well.

§ 250. Biblical dogmatics too comes closer to the statistical method of treating doctrine than to genuine dogmatics.

---

19. On use of the creedal symbols see §§ 98, 211-212, 219-221.

20. The term *historisch* is not to be taken here, or in the next paragraph, in the strict sense of chronicle versus *Geschichte* (see § 153), but in the broader sense of sheer description or depiction versus didactic criticism and construction. See CF §§ 16 and 18. *Historisch* is also the adjective used in the phrase "historical theology," of which dogmatics proper is also a part. Here it is meant in the narrower sense of "historical theology," as applied to the discipline of Church history.

For our manner of construction in dogmatics is very different. On the one hand, reference within biblical dogmatics to the Old Testament canon as a basis for biblical statements in the New Testament is but a very insufficient surrogate for our reference to the New Testament canon in dogmatics proper.[21] On the other hand, biblical dogmatics throughout fails to make us aware of the further developments of later times,[22] which have entered into our convictions to such an extent that we cannot appropriate the material of biblical dogmatics in the manner essential to a genuinely dogmatic treatment. Representing the interconnection of biblical statements in their actual garb is, therefore, a predominantly historical (*historisch*) task. And so, since every comprehensive picture (see § 150) of a period which is posited as a unity actually constitutes the statistics for that period, biblical dogmatics forms only one part of such a picture of the apostolic age.

CONCLUDING REMARKS ON HISTORICAL THEOLOGY

§ 251. In the Christian Church, a preeminent influence of individuals upon the mass is minimal on the whole. Yet it is still more appropriate for historical theology than for other areas of historical study to attach its picture of times which are epoch-making—even if only in a subordinate sense—and which can as such be apprehended as a unity, to the lives of prominently influential individuals.[1]

This influence is minimal because in Christ it was absolute; and to no subsequent individual do we assign an equal position to that of the apostles, recognizing that even among them only a few exercised any decisive personal influence. The further on in history, the more numerous the individuals of any given time by whom any new revolution was effected. This, however, is in no way to be restricted to the age of the so-called "Church fathers." Instead, we might well say that each individual is the more suited to this distinction the more he corresponds to the notion of a "prince of the Church,"[2] but that the further on in history we go the fewer of these are to be expected. It must also be added that particular deviations in doctrine which are noteworthy as indications and anticipations of various kinds are often best understood by reference to the lives of their authors.

§ 252. Knowledge of the historical career of Christianity which must be presupposed for the purposes of philosophical theology (see § 65) need only pertain to chronicle, which is independent of theological study, whereas scientific treatment of this historical career within all the

21. On the canon see §§ 103-109 and index.
22. See §§ 87 and 95.
1. See § 179, also §§ 154 and 199, 312, 323, and 332.
2. See § 9.

branches of historical theology presupposes the results of philosophical theology.[3]

As explained earlier, this is no less true of exegetical and dogmatic theology than of historical theology in the narrower sense. For all their major concepts are definitively determined in those investigations which constitute philosophical theology.

§ 253. This rule, taken together with the present state of philosophical theology (see § 68), serves to explain if not why the working out of all the disciplines of historical theology displays so great a diversity then at least why agreement as to the origin of this diversity is lacking.

For the diversity itself would continue, in any case, because what was said about apologetics in § 51 and extended in § 64 also to polemics must be true not only in respect to the different formations Christianity maintains in different Church communities but also in respect to the not insignificant diversities which exist within each one. If each party has worked out its philosophical theology properly, however, it must also become evident which of these diversities are attached to an original difference in the apprehension of Christianity itself and which are not.

§ 254. Philosophical and historical theology must be still more distinctly separated from each other; nevertheless they can attain completion only with and through each other.

All branches of historical theology suffer from the circumstance that philosophical theology has not yet been worked out in its distinctive character (see § 33). But philosophical theology would become entirely arbitrary if it should detach itself from the obligation to support all its propositions by the clearest historical apprehension possible. Likewise, historical theology would lose all stability if it should refuse to relate itself to the clearest possible development of the elements belonging to philosophical theology.

§ 255. In the present situation, the accusation that a person is doing historical theology according to arbitrary hypotheses may be as easily unreasonable as well-founded.

It is well-founded when the person is seeking to constitute the elements of philosophical theology by sheer construction and is then interpreting his data accordingly. It is unreasonable when the person is making no secret of the fact that his philosophical theology, as it develops for him alongside historical theology, is not verified in itself alone but also according to its suitableness for the work of historical theology.

3. Consult the index under "historical theology" for paragraphs discussing its relations to the other two branches of theology.

§ 256. The same is true for the accusation that a person is converting historical theology into an unintelligent empiricism.

It is well-founded when the person is setting forth as empirically given concepts which are to be cleared through philosophical theology and is then trying to apply them directly to the work of historical theology. It is unreasonable when the person is only protesting against *a priori* construction of these concepts and insisting that critical procedures be used (see § 32).

PART THREE

On Practical Theology

INTRODUCTION

§ 257. Philosophical theology brings clearly to consciousness feelings of pleasure and displeasure concerning the condition of the Church at any given time. It is, accordingly, the task of practical theology to give order to whatever deliberative[1] activity is developed from dispositions associated with such feelings, utilizing what clarity of consciousness has been reached, and to carry this activity to its goal.

Just as philosophical theology is conceived here with regard to the immediate relevance of its results for a particular moment of life, practical theology is also conceived with regard to the immediate applicability of its results within a particular moment of life.

§ 258. Practical theology, therefore, is only for those in whom an ecclesial interest and a scientific spirit are united.

For without an ecclesial interest neither the feelings nor the dispositions just mentioned will arise. And without a scientific spirit no deliberative activity—that is, none which will be guided by precepts—arises either, but rather the sort of motivation which is disinclined toward knowledge and disdains rules.

§ 259. The tasks of any person who is to exert influence of a genuinely deliberative character arise out of the way in which he appraises the actual condition of the Church at the present time, according to his conception of the essence of Christianity and of his own particular Church community.

For since these tasks are, on the whole, identical with those of Church leadership, he can only wish in each instance to make fruitful all that

1. The original for "deliberative" is *besonnene,* in ethical literature sometimes translated "prudential." This connection is significant for §§ 258-259 and 263.

seems to him good and either to make inoperative or to transform what does not.

§ 260. It is not among the aims of practical theology to teach the right conception of these tasks. Rather, presupposing this, it has only to do with correct procedures for executing all the tasks which are to be included within the notion of "Church leadership."[2]

If philosophical and historical theology have been clearly appropriated, and in the right proportion, nothing further remains of a theoretical nature in order to acquire a right conception of these tasks. For then the given situation can also be rightly evaluated in its relation to the aim of Church leadership, and these can thus be set accordingly. Ordinarily, of course, these tasks must also be classified and arranged in certain groupings, always proceeding on the basis of the notion of Church leadership, so that prescriptions for the various practical procedures may be set forth.

§ 261. Some may wish to consider such rules as means toward an end. In this case, on account of the subordination of the means to the end, everything would have to be excluded from these prescriptions which, although it might perhaps have advanced the carrying out of a particular task, still might also have loosened Church ties on the whole or have weakened the force of the Christian principle.

It has become necessary to state this canon because the situation mentioned occurs so frequently. It is patent that any particular good effect following the use of any such means can only be accidental, even if it does not rest upon a sheer illusion, in which case the way in which the task was carried out would certainly not be the right one.

§ 262. Likewise, since an agent can apply his means only with the same disposition by virtue of which he wills the end, no task can be resolved by means which are opposed to either of the two basic elements of the theological disposition.

These two kinds of procedure have shown up in Church practice often enough, i.e., those procedures which run counter to the scientific spirit and those which endanger ecclesial interest in general by falsely appearing to promote it in some particular connection.

§ 263. However, since all deliberative influence upon the Church which is exerted so that Christianity may be more purely represented

2. See the Introduction, especially §§ 3, 5, 7, 11-12, 25-31; also §§ 236, 267n.

within it is nothing other than care of souls (*Seelenleitung*),[3] and since no other means whatever are applicable to this purpose than definite influences upon the hearts of people—thus, again, care of souls: it cannot be fruitful, in view of the fact that means and end completely coincide with each other, to regard these rules as means. They should be regarded simply as methods (*Methoden*).

For means, as such, have to have their place independent of a given end; thus they are not willed in and with the end itself, which can be said here only of what is external in the very highest degree while everything whose place is nearer center is itself contained in the end and constitutes a part of it. This relation of the part to the whole is the most prominent feature of the term "method."

§ 264. The classification of tasks which appear in Church leadership and the specification of procedures can each be traced back to the other.

For every special task is to be regarded, both according to its conception and in its actual occurrence, as part of an overall purpose, namely Church leadership, just as every method to be applied to these special tasks is only a part of this same purpose. Accordingly, these two activities cannot be held apart, as if they were two main divisions of the discipline, since the classification of tasks itself simply serves to specify methods for carrying out the overall task.

§ 265. No prescription of practical theology can be other than a general expression, in which the nature and manner of its application to particular instances is not predetermined; i.e., all these prescriptions are technological rules, or rules of "art" in the narrower sense of the term (see § 132).

In every rule covering a mechanical art, or craft, this application is already provided for, whereas prescriptions belonging to the higher arts are all of the kind mentioned above so that correct practice in conformity to the rules always further requires a special talent whereby one can discover what is right to do.[4]

§ 266. Accordingly, knowing the rules cannot make anyone into a

---

3. Literally the guidance of souls—a peculiarly Christian type of leadership to which Church leadership *(Kirchenleitung)* essentially corresponds in Schleiermacher's scheme.

4. Clarification concerning the different levels of art, only partially distinguished here, must be sought from the lectures on *Aesthetik* (SW III.7). Also compare his definition of Christianity as a teleological, versus aesthetic, religion in CF § 9 (and Addr. 11f). This definition does not mean that Christianity is against art, only that one cannot have a natural flair for it—it must be based in personal relationship and possess ethical content. In Christianity, the natural is subordinated to the moral, whereas in "aesthetic religion" (though not necessarily in art) the opposite relation would obtain.

practical theologian, even supposing that he also has a theological disposition. Rules can only serve as a guide for the person who wants to be a practical theologian and who has the inner constitution and preparation requisite for becoming one.[5]

This is not to say that only very special natural gifts, granted only to a few, equip one for this practical work, nor does it mean that one must be completely prepared before he can decide to pursue it.

§ 267. Christian theology in general, and thus practical theology too, was first capable of development when Christianity had obtained historical importance (see §§ 2-5), and this was possible only by means of the organization of the Christian community. Accordingly, all genuine Church leadership is founded on a distinct formation of the original contrast between prominent members and the mass.[6]

Without such a contrast, capable of the most manifold gradations but grounded in the natural relation of mature persons to the immature, all progressive advance would have to take place within a uniform development of the whole community, never through deliberative leadership.[7] Furthermore, if a distinct formation of this contrast did not exist, leadership could only be a relation between individuals; the community would therefore consist only of free-floating elements and could never operate as a whole, though it is upon this that its historical importance depends.

§ 268. This distinct formation consists in the method of general communication established for the purposes of stabilizing and advancing the community. By virtue of this method the religious force of prominent members rouses the mass, and the mass in turn summons forth such leaders.

That a kind of stabilization should take place in this way and that the mass should gather around prominent persons is natural. Advance, however, is only attainable when the religious force of the whole community is already on the increase, especially among its prominent members.

§ 269. In agreement with all that has gone before,[8] we shall have to

5. First edition: "Thus these, like all technological rules, can only guide, not form, the practitioner."

6. This contrast is further discussed in §§ 278-279, 304-308, 312, 315. Only in § 307 does he first introduce the clergy-laity distinction, which had already been stated here in the first edition. Since his own distinction is out of the ordinary, he no doubt wished to prepare the way before using the traditional terms (only §§ 307 and 315 are completely new in the second edition).

7. See § 257n.

8. Especially §§ 267-268; also see § 279.

give special attention to the formation of this contrast within Christian Church leadership for the purpose of effectively communicating religious ideas and for the purpose of influencing the life of the community, or of conducting common worship and of serving to order and direct morality (*Sitte*).

These do indeed give the appearance of being two separate activities, but according to the formulation here their contrast is actually only partial. For common worship itself exists only as a kind of ordered morality; and since ordering and direction of morality lack all external sanction, their acceptibility simply depends upon effective communication of ideas. This twofold relation nonetheless stands up on its own right.[9]

§ 270. Members are prominent only by virtue of possessing both of the basic elements of the theological disposition,[10] though an exact equilibrium between them is never to be taken for granted. Thus, there is one kind of leadership activity which is more clerical in character and another which is more theological in the narrower sense of the term.[11]

It cannot be shown that this latter differentiation meshes with the preceding one, much less that it subdivides only one member of it. Consequently, both clerical and theological activity are to be regarded, before all else, as overlapping and coordinate.

§ 271. Christianity first became a matter of historical concern[12] when its larger community had come into existence through the joining together of several locally distinct congregations, each of which had given a definite form to that contrast between prominent members and the mass whereby it had originally become a congregation. Thus there came into being activity of leadership whose object is the individual congregation as such and which therefore remains purely local, and also an activity of leadership which is directed toward the whole and whose object is the organic union of congregations, i.e., the Church.

This contrast is also partial, in that something could issue from the leadership of a local congregation which bears upon the whole indirectly, and in that an activity of leadership determined from the standpoint of the whole could happen to affect only a single congregation.

9. See CF § 135 on Word and worship, and see §§ 168-173 above on morality and worship.

10. § 258: i.e., an ecclesial and a scientific interest.

11. This contrast was originally made in § 10.

12. See § 267.

§ 272. In times when the Church is divided, only congregations of one confession are organically united, and distinctive activities of overall leadership are limited to this compass.

To be sure, there are also influences of one Church community upon another; but these cannot have the character of leadership activity.

Even if there were no such division, given the present dispersion of Christianity various external factors would make it impossible to sustain a universal leadership in the Church, one encompassing all the congregations of Christians which exist on this earth.

§ 273. Now it follows that since procedures must be regulated according to the way in which the contrast between prominent members and the mass has been apprehended and brought to form, the theory of Church leadership must also be different for every differently constituted Church community. Thus we are only able to set forth a practical theology for the evangelical Church.

In fact, we cannot even do it for this Church completely, since even here many differences of worship and especially of polity are present. Thus we will direct our attention only to the German evangelical Church.

§ 274. We regard this same contrast, as it was last drawn in § 271, to be the chief ground for dividing up the discipline, and so we call that activity of leadership which is directed toward the whole "Church government" (*Kirchenregiment*) and that which is directed toward the individual local congregation "Church service" (*Kirchendienst*).

It is not as though it lay in the nature of the subject that these should be its main divisions. This division is chosen because it is best fitted to the present situation of our Church. Elsewhere there are circumstances where several congregations are only very loosely bound together, and where little could therefore be said regarding Church government in the sense given here.

Still another way of naming our two divisions suggests itself: if we call the one "Church government" then we might name the other "congregational government." But the above title has been preferred on the same ground for which the corresponding main division was made: because the union of congregations, which we prefer to call "Church," comes to the fore, and it is thus appropriate also to relate the other division to this totality. In this way, then, care for an individual part can only appear as a service which is rendered to the whole.

§ 275. The content of practical theology is exhausted in the theory of

Church government, understood in the narrower sense, and the theory of Church service.

The contrasts specified in §§ 269 and 270 must be taken up and elaborated within these two main divisions.

§ 276. The order of treatment is, in and of itself, of no consequence. We prefer to begin with Church service and to let Church government follow.[13]

It is inconsequential because, in any case, treatment of the antecedent division must still take notice of what is to follow and of the possibility that it might be differently formed.

It is however the natural order that those who are generally suited for any type of Church leadership should begin their public activity in Church service.

I. PRINCIPLES OF CHURCH SERVICE

§ 277. The local congregation, a body of Christian households of the same confession living in the same place and united in a common piety,[14] is the simplest completely ecclesial organization in which leadership activity can take place.

Ordinary language still includes the terms *Landesgemeine* and *Kreisgemeine* [communions or "congregations" extending throughout a nation or district], but here not even a common exercise of piety is always to be found. It also includes *Hausgemeine* [literally, house congregations], only here the leadership activity is not one which proceeds from a distinctly religious interest.[15]

§ 278. If a form of Church service is to exist at all, the contrast between activity which is more influential and that which is more receptive in character must be fixed by agreement, at least for definite moments in the Church's life.

Without such definite moments there can be no common life; and without coming to an agreement over who shall communicate and who receive, this common life would only end in a tangle. Even assuming the greatest similarity among members, division of labor would still be arbitrary; and assuming the greatest dissimilarity, receptivity would still be incumbent upon all.

13. The reverse order was used in the first edition.

14. In Schleiermacher's usage, "piety" means life of faith, thus something more than mere religious belief or practice.

15. The reference is to large communal households, not to "house churches."

The task of determining this relation for each congregation belongs, by the nature of the subject, to Church government.

§ 279. In Church service, leadership activity consists (see § 269) partly in edification, either in common worship or in other assemblies of the congregation for awakening and quickening religious consciousness, and partly of government, which acts not only through the ordering and direction of morality but also through direct influence upon the lives of individual people.

This second aspect could only be designated above (§ 269) in respect to its relation to Church government. Church service, however, would fail in a large part of its task if leadership activity were not also directed toward individuals.

§ 280. Whether edification takes place in Christian worship largely depends upon the process by which religious self-consciousness comes to be thought and then communicated. A theory for all this can be given only insofar as such communication can be regarded as an art.[16]

Indeed, the word "largely" applies to Christianity generally (see § 49), but here especially to evangelical Christianity.

"Thought" is to be taken here in that broader sense in which the elements of poetry are also thoughts. In a certain sense, "art" must be present in any connected train of thought. A theory must always be concerned with both of the following questions: In what degree is art either requisite or allowable here, and by what procedure is the end in view to be attained?

§ 281. The material of common worship, in the narrower sense, can only consist of those ideas which also have their place within the body of Church doctrine. The theory has to determine, therefore, what elements of common doctrine are relevant to this material and in what way they lend themselves to such communication.

Those ideas are "materials," in the narrower sense, which are to be communicated on their own account, as opposed to those which only serve as elucidations and rhetorical aids.

And since these same ideas are worked out in a great variety of ways, from the very popular to the strictly scientific, from the conversational to the oratorical and poetical, it must be determined which of these shades of expression are suited to worship, either in general or in its various aspects.

16. See notes under § 168. In the first edition, the term *Kunstlehre* (technology) is used for the theory of worship.

§ 282. Christian worship, and the evangelical form of it in particular, is compounded of elements pertaining to both prose and poetry. Thus, one must treat first what concerns the form taken by the religious style of speech in its adaptation to Christianity, as it pertains to both prose and poetry; and then one must treat what concerns the form resulting from those various mixtures of the two which may appear in the common worship of evangelical Christianity.[17]

The theory of Church poetry belongs to the doctrine of Church service, at least insofar as all selection from what is already at hand must be made according to the same principles.

§ 283. Uniformity and variety have an unmistakable influence upon the effectiveness of all such modes of communication. Thus the following question is also to be answered: How far, purely out of interest in common worship, must deference to what is already established be sacrificed to better insight, or vice versa?

At first glance, this question seems to belong here only insofar as it can be decided within the congregation itself, without the intervention of Church government. Only since the congregation may still be entirely free in this respect, the whole matter is best dealt with here.

§ 284. Although it is very much in the spirit of the evangelical Church to regard religious discourse as the real core of common worship, yet the form of it which prevails among us today—what we call the "sermon," or "preaching"—is in this particular form something rather uncertain and accidental.

This is sufficiently noticeable from the history of our common worship. It becomes still clearer when one inquires what it is upon which the great inequality in the effectiveness of these discourses actually depends.

§ 285. The discipline which we call "homiletics" normally presupposes this form as established, and relates all its rules principally to it. It would be better, however, to let the restriction go and to treat the subject in a broader and freer manner.

The distinction between the sermon proper and the homily, which began some time ago to be so much noticed that a special theory for the homily has been advanced, is not nearly enough to satisfy the requirement of our proposition.

17. See § 213n.

§ 286. In the evangelical Church, we find common worship consisting almost everywhere of two elements. The one is left entirely to the free productivity of the one who conducts the services; in the other he acts merely as an organ of the Church's government.

In the former element, this person is primarily the "preacher"; in the latter, the "liturgist."

§ 287. The liturgical element can be mentioned here only under the assumption that some freedom for self-determination is still available within it, and only in the degree in which this is the case.

The question regarding self-determination can be decided only from the standpoint of Church government. It could be dealt with here only insofar as it were to be shown that in some instance a total negation of self-determination is opposed to the conception of common worship in the evangelical Church.

§ 288. Since Church service in common worship is essentially tied to certain organic activities which produce an effect while worship is in process, it is to be decided whether and to what extent these activities may also become an object of technological rules; and such rules are to be set forth accordingly.

These rules, then, would be an application of mimicry, in the broader sense of the term, to the area of religious expression.

§ 289. Since the proceedings of Church service are bound within a limited space, which is in its very nature likely to produce some impression while they are going on, it is to be decided to what extent such an impression is allowable or desirable; and rules are to be set forth accordingly.

Since the bounds of this space is only an external factor, and consequently a secondary matter and not a part of worship itself, such rules could only be an application of the theory of decoration to the area of religious expression.

§ 290. If we look solely at the contrast between the more productive and the more receptive within the congregation, in such a way that we view receptivity as fairly equal among its members, then a leadership activity is possible within the congregation of a sort which brings forth something in common. But insofar as any among the receptive lag behind the rest, their condition as individuals becomes a concern for leadership too.

This latter activity is already known by the name of "care of souls" (*Seelsorge*).[18] We begin with this because overcoming such inequality always appears as the primary task. The other we call the regulative, or ordering and directing, activity, which brings the congregation's way of life to the fore as well as particular works done in common.

§ 291. The subjects of pastoral care, in the broader sense, are first of all the children to be educated in the congregation. The theory of that part of Church service whose activity is to be directed toward them is called "catechetics."

As it happens, the name is taken from one form of pastoral practice, and is consequently too limited to stand for the whole compass of this task.[19]

§ 292. The business of catechetics can be rightly ordered only when all participants agree as to when it is to begin and end.

To this extent, therefore, if such an agreement does not arise of itself, both the practice and the theory of catechetics depend upon regulative activity.

§ 293. By virtue of its goal, which is to guide the children into adulthood, so that they may learn to take the receptive rôle as their elders do, catechetical practice must consist of two parts: to help these children become receptive both to the edifying and to the regulative activity of the congregation (see § 279). And this task is to be achieved through one and the same procedure.

The first is the quickening of religious consciousness into thought, and the second is its awakening into motivation for action.[20]

§ 294. However, insofar as the goal should also be to prepare them to be more nearly like those who act mostly on their own initiative, it must be discovered how this can take place without disturbing their relation to the other adults.

---

18. See § 263.
19. Elsewhere he prefers to speak of "Church pedagogics," which relates to the total educational task of the Church.
20. Compare Addr. III-IV.

Catechetics generally reaches back into pedagogics for its technology; so this is also a general pedagogical task, which is nonetheless especially determined in respect to the religious area of education.

§ 295. Since piety is to be developed in both directions (see § 293), not merely in contrast to sensing (*sinnliche*) self-consciousness but also in its Christian and evangelical character,[21] the relation of individual and universal aspects must also be determined here, as to the possibilities both of stabilization and of advance (see § 294[22]).

It is all the more necessary that this task should be taken up in the theory of catechetics, since in recent times the most remarkable errors have arisen at just this point.

§ 296. On similar grounds, those who live within the neighborhood or vicinity of a congregation—as religious strangers, as it were—may also become subjects of a similar activity. This requires a theory of how to deal with converts.

The more definitely the principles of catechetics are set forth the easier it will be to derive this theory from them.

§ 297. However, since this activity is not so naturally grounded certain indications should be drawn up for recognizing whether it is properly motivated.

For it is possible to err in both directions here: in hasty self-confidence and in anxious hesitation.

§ 298. Conditionally, the theory of missions might also be attached here, one which is as good as completely lacking up to the present time.

It could be most easily attached if it were possible to assume that all efforts of this kind are successful only where a Christian congregation is in existence.

§ 299. Those members of the congregation may become special subjects for pastoral care who, from internal or external causes, have lost

---

21. Sensibility, as a lower level of self-consciousness, belongs to one's relatively objective awareness of physical reality external to himself. One's higher, more subjective, religious self-consciousness always includes one's personal association with others, and thus gives rise to the problem of one's relation as an individual to the groups of which he is a part. Ideally, the two "levels" totally overlap, so there is no essential division of human experience. In practice, however, we recognize a tendency for the realm of sense and the realm of love to split apart. Religion or piety is the force which conjoins them. Compare CF §§ 3-5, Addr. 145, and *Soliloquies,* pp. 38-48. These distinctions belong to a highly complex anthropology, developed in the lectures on *Psychologie* (SW III.6).

22. Also see §§ 267-268.

their identification with the rest. Occupation with these persons is called "care of souls" or "pastoral care" (*Seelsorge*) in the narrower sense.

In reality, equality among members, or identification with each other, is always simply the least amount of inequality. Thus those who have the least stable relation with the rest are not meant here, for they are always present. By comparison, the special needs of those referred to here are only occasional.

§ 300. Now since a special relationship is to be formed in this case, the theory must determine first of all whether it can be initiated either by the needy person or by the pastor, or under what circumstances one would be the right approach but not the other.

Up to now, the great variety of ways pastoral care is practiced in different parts of the evangelical Church has not been supported in theory, nor has it been settled in practice.

§ 301. Such a loss of identification which issues from internal causes can only manifest itself in some sort of opposition to the edifying or to the regulative activity of the congregation. Thus it must next be determined whether, according to the spirit of the evangelical Church, the procedure for dealing with such people is to be compounded of both these elements (see § 279), and if so how. Finally, it must also be determined whether pastoral care is always to be regarded as unfinished if it does not achieve its purpose, or whether, and if so when and how far, connection with the leaders of those who have become unreceptive may be regarded as suspended.

The suspension of this connection would automatically require suspension of their connection with the congregation as such.

§ 302. In respect to pastoral care which has become necessary due to external causes, in addition to the first task (see § 300) it is only to be determined how the correspondence of this official activity, which essentially involves looking after the spiritually ill, is to be made with the responsibility to associate with the regular, more receptive members of the congregation.

For the question raised in § 301 can scarcely be disputed at this point, since here it is only a matter of making up for what is neglected through temporary suspension of a person's participation in the common life of the congregation. This kind of edifying activity borders too closely upon ordinary conversation to require a special theory.

§ 303. Regulative activity within the congregation (see § 290) appears limited in its application to morality, partly by the more comprehensive influence of Church government and partly by the irrepressible claims of personal freedom.

One can only say "appears," for leaders should be restrained by their own sense of freedom from intruding into the area of personal freedom. For the same reason, moreover, leaders in Church government ought to be restrained from interfering as centralized authority into areas of decision proper to the congregation alone.

§ 304. As opposed to that of the Roman Catholic Church, evangelical morality, as well as its doctrine, is still very much in process of development. Thus, rules concerning how the common life in any given situation can be brought gradually nearer to a form which corresponds to the more mature insight of its more advanced members can only be set forth in broad scope.

A given situation may still contain within itself various factors carried over from Catholicism which are not yet recognized for what they are. Or it may have erroneously overstepped certain boundaries set by Christianity itself.

§ 305. Since even the life of a Christian congregation is partly determined by social and civil circumstances, it should be specified in what way within this area too, in comparison with others, a more prevalent influence of the Christian and evangelical spirit is to be obtained, insofar as this can result from local factors.

On the whole, only modes of procedure can be dealt with here, in that the substance of ordering activity depends upon the current interpretation of Christian doctrine, especially of Christian ethics.

§ 306. Since any summons to unite forces for the purpose of whatever common efforts lie within the conception and province of a congregation must issue from its ordering activity, it is important to define the limits (see § 303) of such efforts.

The problem is to separate what pertains to official action and persists continuously, e.g., the whole area covered by the diaconate in its original meaning, from what can issue only from the personal relationship of individual leaders toward some part of the whole membership.

§ 307. Church service has been treated here as a single area, without wishing to limit the various possible ways of distributing the responsibilities involved.

Otherwise we would have had to anticipate the theory of Church polity here. At this stage, therefore, we can only follow the old practice of grouping all who undertake the work of Church service under the term "clergy" (*Klerus*).[23]

§ 308. Only in this general way, therefore, can the question be dealt with here as to whether the ecclesial relation between clergy and laity should have any effect upon the association of the two in either civil or social and scientific situations, and if so what kind of effect.

The tasks which are ordinarily treated under the heading of "pastoral discretion" appear as entirely subordinate here. Their resolution depends upon settling the question of whether any difference obtains between members of the clergy who conduct worship and the rest, and if so what difference.

II. PRINCIPLES OF CHURCH GOVERNMENT[24]

§ 309. If Church government is based upon the formation of a central organ within a complex of congregations, then the first task is to note the multiplicity of relations which can develop between Church government and the congregations, and to determine whether there are any forms which are definitely excluded or definitely postulated by the distinctive character of the evangelical Church.

It is presupposed that the formation of such an organ neither contradicts the essence of Christianity nor countermands the free initiative of congregations.

§ 310. The internal Church polity of such a definite complex of congregations is formed in respect to the manner and means by which initiative is taken within it for the exercise of Church government and by which the operation of its government and the free self-determining activity of its congregations mutually stimulate and limit each other. Accordingly, for the evangelical Church the above-mentioned task tends to be carried out by referring back to certain basic principles which touch upon both its multiplicity of forms and its contrast to the Roman Catholic Church.

23. See §§ 236 and 267n.
24. For earlier principles see §§ 5, 277-279, 283, 286-287, 303.

On the one hand, the results of this work must derive from propositions of dogmatics. On the other hand, successful results can be obtained only by making appropriate use of Church history and Church statistics.

§ 311. Since the evangelical Church does not at present form a single complex of congregations, and since within different complexes the internal polity is also different even though its theology is supposed to be the same for all, therefore the theory of its Church government must set its own tasks in such a way that they are the same for all possible evangelical polities and can be carried out in respect to each one.

The qualifier "at present" is only intended to indicate that the impossibility of any outward unity for the whole evangelical Church is, at the very least, not predetermined.

§ 312. Since every historical whole can endure only through the same forces by which it has originated, evangelical Church government accordingly consists of two elements: the "binding" or authoritative, i.e., the formation of a basic contrast [between the governing and the governed, or the clergy and the laity[25]] within any given complex, and the discretionary, i.e., any free influence upon the whole, which any individual member of the Church may undertake who believes himself called to do so.

The evangelical Church originated out of this kind of free influence, with regard not only to its certification of doctrine but also to its polity or authoritative Church government. Without this influence, moreover, no improvement of its polity could conceivably take place, since binding or authoritative Church government is identical with its conception of polity.

Should the second element appear to give rise to disorderly government, one should only bear in mind that if a person believes himself to be called to exercise influence but is not among the most productive people of the Church, his effort would of itself come to nothing.

§ 313. These two elements can only have the same aim (see § 25): ever more authentically to represent the idea of Christianity within the evangelical Church according to that Church's distinctive conception of it, and to gain increasingly greater support for this idea. The organized element, i.e., the ecclesial power or—more correctly—authority, is in a position to serve this aim by means of ordinance or restriction, however,

25. From the first edition. See §§ 307 and 267n.

while the unorganized element or free spiritual power[26] can only operate by means of stimulus and warning.

Yet it is to be understood that the ecclesial power also lacks any external sanction for its declarations. Thus the difference essentially comes to this: that these declarations operate as an expression of the present spirit and disposition of the community,[27] while the free spiritual power seeks to bring something new into this communal disposition and spirit.

§ 314. The condition of a given whole within the Christian Church is the more satisfactory the more vitally both sorts of activity affect each other and the more definitely action in both areas is accompanied by a consciousness of their contrast.

Ecclesial authority, therefore, has to combine the following two aims, and the theory of Church government must try to find the corresponding formula (see § 310): to preserve and strengthen the principle which was formed during the preceding epoch (its main duty), and also, at the same time, to tender and protect expressions of free spiritual power, which alone can initiate reforms. Furthermore, some indication should be given as to how free spiritual power can be content with what may be achieved through the auspices of ecclesial authority without sacrificing its strength of conviction.

§ 315. Since a larger ecclesial fellowship can exist only where there is a certain degree of parity among its constituent congregations, or a certain facility in attaining accommodation to each other, thus the ecclesial authority has an overall part in the process of forming and maintaining the contrast between the clergy and the laity within the congregations.

But only a part, because the congregation exists prior to any broader ecclesial ties[28] and because it is what it is only insofar as this contrast obtains within it.

§ 316. Since the part the ecclesial authority plays here can vary from a maximum to a minimum degree of influence, the theory of Church government first has to fix the range of influence and then to determine for what different conditions and circumstances each mode of influence is applicable and whether this should vary or be the same for all functions of Church service.[29]

---

26. See § 152n.
27. See § 180n.
28. See § 277.
29. On the relation of Church government and Church service see § 274.

For if one refers to any and all similar situations it becomes obvious that within this apparently continuous span from minimum to maximum influence certain major break-off points can still be distinguished.

§ 317. Furthermore, since this parity cannot be regarded as either inalterable or self-sustaining, but must, by consequence, be a work of the ecclesial authority as well, thus the manner and means by which this influence is to be exercised, i.e., the notion of ecclesial legislation, should be determined.

The term "as well" is used because this parity must already exist in some sense prior to the ecclesial authority.

The term "legislation" must remain inexact, inasmuch as the ecclesial authority likewise dispenses with all external sanction.

§ 318. Now since this parity only becomes immediately apparent in common worship and in morality,[30] and since both ought to be in themselves the sufficient expression of the prevailing piety of each locality, the task thus arises of conjoining the two by means of ecclesial legislation and of keeping them conjoined.

It is of the nature of the case that this end can only be approximated, and that the theory of Church government must therefore chiefly seek to confine fluctuation between the preponderance of one or other of these two elements within the narrowest possible bounds.

§ 319. Since both common worship and morality continue to be expressions of Church unity only insofar as each retains some identity, and in view of the fact that everything which is an expression or means of representing something, insofar as it is this, gradually changes in its actual significance, the legislative task thus arises of giving specific recognition to the freedom and mobility of both while also confirming the overall uniformity of both.

At the same time, this procedure will also at least confine within certain bounds the relation of ecclesial authority to Church service in the process of constituting common worship and morality.

§ 320. Furthermore, in case of strife within the congregation, whether it comes from individuals who have fallen out of fellowship with the whole (see § 299) or from a more general failure of unity, it must be within the competence of the ecclesial authority, as the highest expression

30. See §§ 166-173, 269.

of the spirit of the whole community, to make a decision if no agreement can be achieved within the congregation itself.

Such a decision will have real value only insofar as the contenders are also willing to continue seeking to satisfy their impetus to Christian community within this particular fellowship of the Church.[31]

§ 321. Insofar as the ecclesial authority does intervene, either through general regulations or in applying them to individual cases, the issue must be settled here as to whether special disciplinary penalties or perhaps even excommunication are to be permitted within a fellowship of the evangelical Church, and if so under what circumstances.

The question of excommunication applies insofar as it is possible for the ecclesial authority to terminate the relation of a person to a congregation or larger fellowship. The question of special discipline applies insofar as it is supposed that where opposition has arisen it can only be brought to an end by a person's public acknowledgment of its falsity.

§ 322. Concerning the relation of the ecclesial authority to the system of doctrine held by the Church, views of such a contradictory nature still prevail that it seems impossible to find a common starting-point. Thus, a corresponding theory can be set forth only conditionally.

Indeed, it would not even be easy to bring the various parties to an agreement over the place where the controversy ought to be decided—and consequently, as it were, to bring them to the choice of an arbitrator.

§ 323. Recognizing on the one hand that evangelical Church union has arisen with the contention—or almost out of it—that no given authority is competent either to determine or to alter the Church's system of doctrine, and recognizing on the other hand that, irrespective of the plurality of evangelical Church unions, which tend to follow different rules, we still acknowledge the existence of one evangelical Church and one doctrinal fellowship attesting this unity, we find ourselves in a position to set our task only in the following manner. Noting that changes in doctrinal statements and formulas may result from the study of individuals only when such changes have been received as part of the conviction of a congregation, it is to be determined how the ecclesial au-

31. See §§ 299-301. On the impetus to community, compare §§ 55-57, 166.

thority of each union may serve to enable free spiritual power to have influence and yet at the same time hold fast to the unity of the Church according to its originating principles.

By this it is of course by no means intended to exclude the possibility that those who exercise ecclesial authority may also bear influence through free study. It must be insisted all the more strongly, however, that they must not do this as an expression of ecclesial authority or under its aegis.

The task here must be set in an entirely opposite way if we proceed from the presupposition that the Church's unity is maintained only by an exactly specifiable uniformity of doctrine.

§ 324. What was stated above (in § 322) also applies to the rights and obligations of the ecclesial authority in respect to the relations of Church and State, since no manner of procedure which could be prescribed would enjoy general acknowledgment.

Only the following appears to be notable at this point: that where the evangelical Church is wholly separate from the State no one wishes it to be otherwise, but where a closer tie exists between the two there is a division of opinion within the Church.

§ 325. Assuming on the one hand that if the Church does not intend to be a secular power it must also be unwilling to be mixed up in the organization of secular power, and assuming on the other hand that what those members of the Church who have high positions in civil government do within the ecclesial area they can do only in the form of Church leadership, we are able to set our task only in the following manner. Under various given circumstances, it is to be determined in what way the ecclesial authority has to work in order to keep the Church from falling either into a powerless sort of independence from the State or into a kind of servitude, however respectable, under the State.

The theory which applies here is extremely difficult to set forth, and in any case yields but little profit. For if the ecclesial authority has to work with either a fusion of the Church with the political organization or a mode of procedure in ecclesiastical affairs by which the influence of external sanctions is allowed, it can only indirectly counteract this under its own form of organization and must expect any further change to come only through the gradual influence of free spiritual power.

Furthermore, how little agreement there is even regarding basic principles is most clearly seen in the fact that where the Church is in a state of servitude without respectability, some will always prefer to acquire distinction in servitude, while others prefer to remain without consequence if they can only attain independence thereby.

§ 326. If the State has taken up the entire organization of educational institutions into its own organization, the same task arises again, though in a special relation, since a like threat of powerless independence or prosperous servitude appears in relation to that spiritual culture by which evangelical worship can alone be maintained and without which a free spiritual power cannot persist within the Church.

For this area of concern, the following dilemma may very easily develop under unfavorable circumstances; it is a difficult one, and the path to its solution is not simple to find: namely, whether a Church body shall be contented with such apparatus, however meager, as it is able independently to obtain and preserve, or whether it shall venture to draw also from sources in which there is an admixture of nonevangelical elements.

§ 327. The various discrete unions of congregations which together form the evangelical Church are all limited partly by external factors subject to change and partly by differences in ethics or doctrine whose value is also subject to change; most of these unions, however, find their autonomy endangered by this limiting process. Consequently there arises for each of them the task of keeping itself open to a closer relationship with the rest and of preparing the way within itself so that it will not let slip any favorable opportunity of calling forth such a relationship.

This task also marks the boundary line of ecclesial authority, for not only does every previous Church government become extinct, as far as any separate existence is concerned, once this task is carried out, but the very execution of this task can only be called forth through the agency of free spiritual power, since it extends beyond the area of isolated authority.

§ 328. The discretionary element of Church government (see § 312), which we designate as "free spiritual power" within the evangelical Church, a power which we take to be an activity of individuals directed toward the whole body, presupposes the existence of a public life as free from limitation as possible, so that the individual can express himself. Accordingly, at the present time this element is especially to be found within the vocation of the academic theologian and of Christians who write on matters concerning the Church.

"Academic theologian" is not intended to suggest only the form of lecturing, though oral communication which, in many ways, bears a decisive influence upon the large number of youth who are destined to the work of Church leadership will always be greatly desirable.

The other vocation does not include in this connection those who only commit to writing their various contributions to ordinary Church service.

§ 329. Persons who follow these two vocations will achieve their most general influence (see §§ 313, 314) only insofar as they approximate the notion of a "prince of the Church" (see § 9).[32]

The more what they produce is restricted to their use of particular scientific skills, the less need either of them has for that balance [between a religious interest and a scientific spirit] referred to in § 9—but also the less success either will have in exercising any general and decisive influence upon Church government.

§ 330. Since the academic instructor, in dealing with youth who are especially motivated by religious interest, has to bring the theological aspect of the scientific spirit to their awareness for the first time, the method is thus to be specified by which this spirit may be quickened in them without weakening their religious interest.

How little we are as yet in possession of such a method may be learned from experience, of a sort which happens only too often. For the rest, it remains undecided whether this method should be a general one or whether it should derive from different considerations for different disciplines.

§ 331. Since available knowledge is all the less sufficient the more the individual disciplines are penetrated by the scientific spirit, a mode of procedure should be set forth whereby the advancement of the theological sciences may be encouraged and directed, while providing for a correct evaluation of their previous results and a faithful preservation of whatever of lasting value has been deposited thereby within the Church.

A similar experience confirms the same lack here. Undeniably, much of that all-too-sharp split between those who advocate the new and those who submit to the old must be credited to the current method of instruction.

---

32. See also § 258.

§ 332. Insofar as writing is directed toward combating what is false and destructive, a method is to be specified, particularly for the theological writer, whereby he may not only discover but also obtain recognition for the true and good to which that which is false and corrupt is found attached, and whereby he may likewise show the relation of whatever distinctive situation in which these appear to the needs of the Church.

The principle that all error exists only in respect to the truth and that all that is bad exists only in respect to the good is the basic condition of all controversy and of all correction.

The last-mentioned part of this task rests on the one hand upon the presupposition that unless erroneous and destructive factors are conveyed through some distinctive situation, such factors are incapable of exerting much influence. On the other hand this task rests on the presupposition that in the Church every gift may yield something for the benefit of the whole community.

§ 333. Insofar as the task here is to recommend and to obtain recognition for what is new, a formula must be found indicating how exhibition of the contrast between the old and the new, and of their interconnection, may be undergirded most effectively.

For if there were no such contrast, nothing would be new, and if there were no such interconnection, nothing new could be conjoined to what has already existed.

§ 334. Since it is easy for public communications to spread beyond the circles in which they are properly understood, the further task arises of disposing every such presentation in such a way that it shall have a special attraction only for those who may be expected to make a correct use of it.

The rule which was formerly, almost exclusively, recommended and applied for this purpose is no longer adapted to present circumstances: that is, the rule that only "the learned language" [Latin[33]] should be used for presentations which could readily be misinterpreted or misused.

CONCLUDING REMARKS ON PRACTICAL THEOLOGY

§ 335. There could be no mention here of the distinction between what is obligatory for every theologian and what constitutes a specialty.

---

33. In Germany, some theological and Church documents were still being written in Latin. For his understanding of "theological language" see CF §§ 16-18 and 5:P.S.

For the distinction can be based only on limitations which are contingent to given circumstances, or even virtually personal, and for this reason it arises quite on its own. From a general standpoint, every person who is called to the work of Church leadership can become effective in every function discussed under this heading. It is not so much distinctly different areas which are significant here, but rather the varying degrees of accomplishment which can be attained.

§ 336. The tasks of practical theology, especially in the area of Church government, will be most accurately stated by the person who has most thoroughly and completely developed his philosophical theology. The most appropriate methods will occur to the person whose historical basis for living in the present is the deepest and most diversified. The execution of these methods must be promoted, for the most part, by means of a person's natural talents and his general culture.

If not everything which is delineated within the entire encyclopedic outline were required here, the outline itself would be incorrect. The requirement of everything would likewise be incorrect if it embraced anything incapable of being contained within such an encyclopedic outline.

§ 337. The present condition of practical theology shows that what comes at the end of a theological student's training also appears at the end of the general development of theology.

This is so if only because it presupposes the thoroughgoing development of philosophical theology (see §§ 66, 259).[34]

§ 338. Since in the evangelical Church both Church service and Church government are essentially conditioned by this Church's opposing position vis-à-vis the Roman Church, it is the highest accomplishment of practical theology to fashion both aspects of Church leadership in a way which shall be best adapted to the present state of this opposing position as compared with its culminating point historically.

This task relates especially to the supreme task of apologetics (see § 53).

34. Also § 85.

EDITOR'S POSTSCRIPT

PART I. PHILOSOPHICAL THEOLOGY

Apart from his Introduction to *The Christian Faith*, Schleiermacher never lectured on philosophical theology itself. None of his other writings fits his own definition of it. Yet there is clear evidence in nearly all his extant works that he had formulated a highly developed position. By habit, he was continually reworking this complex philosophical material in his head as he set himself to other related tasks with his pen. In this way, this thought developed gradually and smoothly in many fields over several decades, the whole process taking place within a fairly consistent framework of basic concepts. The product was superbly rational, but at the same time remarkably nonrationalistic.

Why, then, did he produce no fully organized lectures on philosophical theology, either for the public or for his students? One reason was that he believed its actual subject matter had "already been worked up fairly completely," so that the distinctive nature of Christianity could be identified and many concepts important for the rest of theology defined. Another ground, of even greater significance here, was that "such a discipline . . . has thus far never been exhibited or recognized as a unit; and the reason is that the need for it, as it is conceived here, first arises only with the problem of organizing the theological sciences" (§ 24; see §§ 29, 68, 180, 252-253). The field was not yet mature enough for him to give a public demonstration of it. He wisely chose rather to work toward its development by pointing unmistakably to the need. As a result, the impact of what he accomplished has been reverberating through the halls of theological learning ever since.

Insofar as theological studies remain disorganized, however, the message he tried to put across has probably not yet been clearly heard. For he was surely right in supposing that as long as scholars are indifferent to the task of interrelating all the theological disciplines, they will not recognize the need for that careful definition of the basic terms of theological discourse which philosophical skills alone can provide. The propagation of Christianity does not depend on reason alone, of course, but is essentially transmitted in personal encounter. Schleiermacher's reasoned insistence on this fact in the *Addresses on Religion* probably made him more famous than all his other deeds put together, but it constitutes, at most, only a third of his actual contribution to modern thought. Another third was his definition of the essence of Christianity, unfolded throughout the whole extent of *The Christian Faith* and both supplemented and supported in his other theological works. The final third was his calm, coolheaded attempt to bring order into the process of attaining knowledge, in many areas, both theological and nontheological.

Nontheological knowledge Schleiermacher generally divided into two parts: that pertaining to the distinctively human, which he called "ethics" or the *Geisteswissenschaften,* and that pertaining to the natural world, which he called "physics" or the *Naturwissenschaften.* Of all the theological disciplines, philosophical theology is most closely related to ethics, the latter being understood as an organization of knowledge representing the whole of human culture, not morality alone.

Largely because of this close relation to ethics, Schleiermacher was able to state that "everyone's philosophical theology essentially includes within it the principles of his whole theological way of thinking" (§ 67). Ethics, in his view, is the science of the human, the science of the principles of history. Within its own proper sphere, philosophical theology considers what it means for Christians to do theological science, the science of God's history with man. Philosophical theology answers to the irrepressible need for clarity as to what the distinctive nature of Christianity is over against other kinds of human experience. Thus, without accepting one single strictly philosophical proposition in the statement of Christian doctrine and ethics (see CF § 2), he could nonetheless admit that all the "major concepts" of historical theology "are definitively determined in those investigations which constitute philosophical theology" (§ 252). This is true, purely and simply, because theology is a human enterprise. It is more than that, for it is reflection upon God's presence with his people; but the human element can never be excised. In Christ, the human is perfectly affirmed. In him, our humanity is redeemed and reconciled to God. Through the regeneration and the sanctification he alone brings, the creation of human nature is brought toward its consummation. Christian theology is the Church's ordered reflection on that twofold fact of God's history with the human world.

This latter definition of theology accounts for two important elements of Schleiermacher's own theological way of thinking. First, it accounts for his insistence that independent philosophical thought is totally off-bounds to Christian theology, though in the end some of it may not be contradictory to what theology affirms. Second, it accounts for the ability of theology to make use, as he often does, of untraditional forms of thought, derived from every area of human experience, without allowing these to become sources for the substance of Christian thought.

It will be noted that his use of the terms "apologetics" and "polemics" for the two parts of philosophical theology practically reverses ordinary usage. In no sense is apologetics, for Schleiermacher, an attempt to defend, prove, or sell Christianity to outsiders. It is only an attempt to clarify, in general terms recognizable to insiders and outsiders alike, what Christianity is. Polemics, on the other hand, is entirely directed to the detection of diseased conditions within Christianity itself.

On this view of apologetics and polemics, every branch of the Christian Church has the responsibility of developing its own philosophical theology, but the scope of this task also requires that provisions be made toward the breaking down of radical disunity within the one Church (see § 53). As such, philosophical theology may well be regarded as the one great undeployed weapon of the ecumenical movement. It is clearly an internal discipline of the Church. It was not created to satisfy independent philosophical interests. It came into being in order to enable historical theology to operate more honestly, more efficiently, and therewith more convincingly, in view of the diverse and divided state of the one Church (see §§ 27-28, 65, 254-255). Consequently, it has a preeminently ecumenical function, in the ordinary current understanding of ecumenical as that which serves to unite the Church in its total life.

PART II. HISTORICAL THEOLOGY

For Schleiermacher, historical theology provides the core curriculum for a well-grounded theological education. Few encyclopedists have followed his subdivision of the field into exegetical theology, Church history, and contemporary theology (including dogmatics and statistics), but his reasons for gathering the three under the heading "historical theology" are not easily circumvented. The first reason was that every leader in the Church ought to have some knowledge of the history of Christianity—its origins, its past, and its present condition, embracing in each period both its communal life and its doctrine. Other reasons appear in his description of the three major areas of study, each of which has a unique theological task in its own right (compare CF § 19: P.S.), and of their relation to philosophical theology on the one hand and to practical theology on the other.

A second underlying reason for calling all these disciplines "historical theology" will become immediately apparent. It is Schleiermacher's view that overemphasis of either an empirical or a speculative method of understanding Christianity detracts from the radically concrete, historical reality of God's presence within the Church, from the Incarnation until now. No history—no people of God. No people—no Christianity. No Christianity, understood as the definite history of a people, of their roots, their traditions, and their present experience—no theology. Much of the current bewilderment of theologians and students of theology alike is perhaps due to their inability to identify with a particular Christian people, and thereby to their inability to find themselves within a definite history. If nothing else, Schleiermacher's outline clearly indicates at what an enormous cost the predicament is maintained.

PART II, SECTION I. EXEGETICAL THEOLOGY

Within Schleiermacher's threefold scheme, exegetical theology brings us "the knowledge of primitive Christianity," primarily through an intimate acquaintance with documents written by early Christians (see §§ 83-85, 88). Although exegetical theology provides philosophical theology with historical material necessary for separating out the distinctive nature of Christianity from that of other faiths, it does not simply elaborate on what it has already provided for that purpose (see §§ 85, 252). Nor, on the other hand, does it simply show how Christianity began. The New Testament writings are an essential, contemporary feature of the Church's life in any age, because they contain Christ's own proclamation of himself and of the kingdom of God, and because they contain the testimony of those directly influenced by him. We turn to these Scriptures for the formation of our own doctrine, and for its testing, moreover, not because we first assume their divine inspiration and authority but because we want to understand what he did and said. By that same Spirit who enlivened and illumined the early Christian community, we are enabled to discover him too. This is how we attain conviction about the authority of Scripture. We do not begin the other way around. (See CF §§ 127-132 for Schleiermacher's doctrine of Scripture, followed by the doctrine of the Ministry of the Word of God in §§ 133-135; also see CF §§ 14:P.S. and 27. Compare Addr. 181, 249, 264.)

The primary task of exegetical theology, therefore, is to make the New Testament accessible to the Church, so that Christ may disclose himself to us as he did to his earliest disciples. "The grounds of faith must be the same for us as for the first Christians" (CF § 128:2,592). Christian faith is a saving relationship to God through the past and present mediation of Christ. Coming to an understanding about our faith does not require that we mimic Scripture, only that we try to understand what Scripture says. For this purpose, knowledge of the past experience of the Church, through Church history, and of present experience, through dogmatics and Church statistics, will be helpful. To exclude such knowledge would be seriously detrimental. Nevertheless, Scripture must also be approached on its own grounds, within the conditions of its own history. Exegetical theology utilizes no other rules of hermeneutics and criticism than would be applicable to other writings, but it adapts them to the special historical conditions of Holy Scripture. Once it is relieved of the mistaken duty of providing proof texts for belief, by rather seeking to understand the whole canon, and each document within it as a whole, it can proceed as a bona fide philological discipline without surrendering its theological character. (See CF § 130: 2,600, and § 121 and note here.)

In Schleiermacher's view, hermeneutics—the art of understanding what documents say—had scarcely begun to develop into an integrated discipline. General progress toward a more adequate and cohesive theological method depended to a large extent on the development of this art, which in turn demanded thorough philosophical investigation. Unfortunately, his own mature thinking on the subject is only lightly reflected in this outline. This thinking rests, among other things, upon his extensive practical experience in interpreting Greek philosophy, in translating nearly the whole of Plato's works, in producing several lengthy studies in New Testament criticism, in preparing sermons regularly over more than three decades, and in offering exegesis courses on all the New Testament books except Revelation. Student notes from the hermeneutics lectures of 1826-1827, 1828-1829, and 1832-1833 are contained in SW I.7, together with those on philological criticism, given concurrently. Texts solely from Schleiermacher's own hand have been gathered in a new critical edition, *Hermeneutik,* by Heinz Kimmerle (Heidelberg, 1959). This includes his influential addresses of 1829, "Ueber den Begriff der Hermeneutik," also to be found in SW III.3,344-386. All this work forms a methodological counterpart to the present outline, which centers attention on problems of organizing theological studies, and is extraordinarily relevant to current discussion on hermeneutics.

The timeliness of his critical work in exegesis is also to be seen in the importance he attributed to the historical Jesus. He gave courses on "The Life of Jesus" five times between 1819 and 1832. The lectures edited in SW I.6 are primarily from 1832.

Old Testament studies were still in their infancy during Schleiermacher's lifetime, which partly explains his de-emphasis of these writings (see § 115 and note; also see CF §§ 12, 27:3, and 132). No doubt he would make much more of them today, and his exposition of doctrine would have to change accordingly. It remains integral to his position, however, that the New Testament writings should be granted unique standing and authority over against all others.

PART II, SECTION II. CHURCH HISTORY

Church history, as Schleiermacher sees it, is not a subdivision of world history, but a theological discipline employing historical method in order to depict a special history. It presupposes that the advent of Christ has inaugurated a new period in world history. Its task, however, is not to show what effect this event has had upon the world in general but to portray the continuing impact of the Holy Spirit upon the Church's own life and doctrine as it lives in the world (see §§ 188, 180 and notes; compare CF § 126 and SW I.11, 15f). Appropriately, the heading he gives to his doctrine of the Church in *The Christian Faith* is "The Constitution of the World in Relation to Redemption" (CF §§ 113-163). That is what Church history is about too.

Schleiermacher offered a survey course on Church history at least three times, in 1806, 1821-1822, and 1825-1826. A lengthy (and not entirely trustworthy) transcript from student notes has been published in SW I.11, including a 47-page introduction on his theological assumptions and on questions of method. Schleiermacher's only substantial published work on Church history was translated into English by Moses Stuart, with extensive notes: "On the Discrepancy between the Sabellian and Athanasian Method of Representing the Doctrine of the Trinity," *The Biblical Repository and Quarterly Observor* 5 (April 1835), 34-353, 6 (July 1835), 1-116.

His fullest summary statement on historical method as applied to Church history is given in the present outline. To understand his theological assumptions adequately, however, one must consider his entire doctrine of the Church. The portion presented in CF §§ 126 and 148-156 is most directly relevant. For further clarification, one must turn to his studies on philosophical ethics and Christian ethics, from which the basic elements of this statement are derived.

For the most part, what he says here is clear enough by itself. The great challenges come in trying to fulfill his terrific demands for thorough theological grounding, ecumenical perspective, and apt historical focus in the work of Church history, or in taking seriously his dialectic between internal and external factors in the history of the Christian community, or in discerning the proper relation between Church history and the history of science and politics, or in separating the diseased from the healthy, the mutable from the immutable, and the individual from the communal. The challenges come, furthermore, in holding to the unusually close interrelations between morality and worship, ethics and polity, doctrine and life, to which he points here. In sum, the task is to produce authentic history rather than chronicle—or as nonspecialists to look for it—and to do so in such a way that the practical needs of the Church are served.

PART II, SECTION III. DOGMATICS AND STATISTICS

Schleiermacher's Dogmatics, *The Christian Faith,* was the only large-scale theological work he was able to publish before his sudden death at age sixty-five in 1834. It represented the subject to which he gave the greatest priority in his teaching, alongside Christian ethics, and which is the culminating point in his outline of theological studies. Dogmatics is the culminating point because here all one's labors in other disciplines come to their fruition and test.

Of course, even Christian thought, for Schleiermacher, rests not on intellection alone but on a combination of intuition and feeling—an immediate awareness of God's presence within the fellowship of Christians, transforming and motivating one's innermost being. Yet the whole environment of a person—including his own body (and, from a Christian viewpoint, centering upon God's decisive world-forming, community-forming, person-forming activity in Christ)—is inseparably conjoined within the texture of one's inner experience, giving it direction and the means of concrete expression. Even deep within, one's spiritual awareness has an external origin, because it is affected by God's own action in history and is coupled with one's objective awareness of the world and of other people.

A person has the capacity to grasp and to express truth *in terms his environment provides.* That is what the intuition aspect of religious consciousness means. The feeling aspect refers to a person's capacity both to receive and to respond to what God offers, *out of his own inner self.* Thus, the term Schleiermacher ordinarily uses for the place in which authentic doctrine arises is "religious self-consciousness," understood as a person's genuine awareness of God out of his own inner self. His shorthand expression for a person's relation to God is "the feeling of absolute dependence," for even one's capacity to absorb and to act, though relatively free, is originated and sustained by God, is fundamentally, thoroughly conditioned by God's work of creation and redemption. On the one hand, we are in no instance totally determined, else we could not even feel our dependence. On the other hand, our freedom is always limited, because it is always in some respect related to the divine government of the world. Schleiermacher insisted with equal force on both points, and both are essential for understanding his approach to problems of religious communication. (See CF § 4, but in the context of the whole discussion of §§ 3-19. Consistent with his interpretation, Schleiermacher seldom uses the general, shorthand phrase in the explicit exposition of Christian doctrine in Part Two of the CF.)

Schleiermacher's own awareness of these matters, though he was able to express it in philosophical terms, arose out of his experience within the Christian community. It had a concrete, historical referent: that community's own inner experience of God's action in the continuing self-communication of Jesus the Redeemer within their midst. There was one authentic origin of their faith—God. There was one genuine source of their life and doctrine—Jesus. There was one basic history within which they could become disciples of Jesus and heirs of the first Christians—the history of the Church. No purely objective authority or sanction could provide security for their faith, however, not even the New Testament. The canon of their belief had to be sought within the New Testament, taken as a whole, which then became authoritative over against all other sources, including their own predispositions, because its message had begun to be validated within their own experience—in the demonstration of the Spirit and with power.

There is no such thing, in Schleiermacher's view, as a feeling of absolute dependence without concrete reference. There is no such thing as a "natural" religious expression of this feeling, lacking specific historical roots and context. Christianity is the highest, final expression of that feeling, because, or insofar as, it rests in God's own revelation of himself in Christ. The Church, moreover, is the place where that feeling is best fed, tested, and perfected, for this is where Christ continues to be at work among a people, without which no secure reception or expression of God's work among men is possible. There the feeling of absolute dependence becomes the "basic consciousness" that "we have fellowship with God only in a living fellowship with the Redeemer" (CF § 91), and this correspondingly takes place only through the fellowship of Christ's people.

It is because, in view of such conditions, Christianity is the most historical, the most communal-, person-, and action-oriented, and likewise the most intellectual of religions, that dogmatics is necessary. Obviously, the mission of Christianity does not solely depend on the results of intellectual endeavor. Without it, however, the Church lives in confusion over its own origin and history, its own present condition, and the function of its total mission within God's purpose for the world. All theological disciplines have the responsibility of using rigorous historical-critical methods. Dogmatics has the task of using these for the cohesive presentation of doctrine now capable of validation within the current experience of the Church. As such, it is the scholarly servant of proclamation, in all its forms: of preaching, but also of the whole vast field of Christian action covered by ethics and practical theology.

Schleiermacher did not much care for any of the titles normally applied to this discipline. "Dogmatics" carried with it a pejorative connotation and the false suggestion that doctrine must be derived from classic confessions, and not merely referred to them with special deference (as was his practice). It thus tended to detract from the contemporary focus of the work, its open contact with the world outside the institutional Church, and its especially scientific character. "Systematic theology" pointed to the scientific character of the discipline (he did not restrict "scientific" to methods used by the natural sciences); but it concealed the historical character of the discipline and its relation to Church leadership (see §§ 97-99, 249-250; also CF §§ 1 and 19). The only solution was to use the terms and let their meaning become clear through actual practice.

Church statistics, designed to provide knowledge of the present condition of the Church, was a new discipline in the early nineteenth century (see § 95n). Schleiermacher was among the first to lecture on the subject. Today the discipline he outlined exists in only scattered fashion—in periodicals covering current events, in books on "the present situation," in works on ecumenics, worship, polity, and social ethics, in sociological studies, in conference reports, and in the annual reports of Churches. Principles for the relation of Church statistics to dogmatic theology have been set forth here in §§ 166-183 and § 195. Symbolics, a comparative study of doctrinal standards and their use (see § 249 and index), may also be included in Church statistics. In any case, no radical separation between doctrine and life is allowed.

In the light of Schleiermacher's outline, it is astounding to find that a great part of the work on "contemporary theology" at present follows the pattern of Church statistics. Dogmatics, including Christian ethics, has often become a collection of current ecclesial themes rather than an ordering perspective rooted in history. Consequently, practical theology, though advancing by leaps and bounds in many other respects, has often become a congeries of techniques largely lacking in firm theological grounding. A key methodological question today, for professional and beginning student alike, is whether a viable alternative to present practice can be achieved in our situation.

PART III. PRACTICAL THEOLOGY

"Practical theology is the crown of theological study," said Schleiermacher in the first edition. This high evaluation is consistent with his notion of theology as the servant of Church leadership. Previous work in this discipline too had been "extremely erratic" (see § 25). Here, as in his lectures on the subject, given six times between 1821 and 1833 (SW I.13), he has accepted his own challenge to put proper order into it.

The whole of Schleiermacher's practical theology stands under the proviso that "we posit the planting and extension of the Christian Church as the object of the divine government of the world" (CF § 164). His interpretation of what this means for the Church's life in the modern world is one of the most exciting and timely contributions of his theology. In the present outline, the sections on Christian education, evangelism, and mission would have to be much longer today. (See his remarks in §§ 296-298.) His own views on education were developed in his famous lectures on *Pädagogik* (SW III.9), from 1813-1814, 1820-1821, and 1826. Relevant material is also to be found in his Christian ethics and in most of his other writings. His understanding of mission and evangelism is stated in CF §§ 106-125 and §§ 164-169 (compare Addr. V).

A second major theme of importance for our own situation is his notion that Church leadership is essentially care of souls (see § 263). In his view, the most menial administrative task in the Church ought to bear this character. That care of souls is not relegated to the clergy alone within the Christian community, but is, in a variety of ways, a responsibility of all Christians points to much territory in the area of "lay ministry" which is still largely unexplored. (For example, consider § 308 in its context.)

Of supreme importance is the connection Schleiermacher envisaged between practical theology and the other theological disciplines. The subject matter and task of practical theology are first fixed through the apologetical and polemical constructions of philosophical theology (§§ 66, 257-259, 336; for example, note the relation of apologetics to evangelism suggested in § 39). Without philosophical theology, the basic areas of concern which belong to practical theology cannot be properly identified. Its doctrinal foundation is in the whole of historical theology, without which its rules "can only have the effect of a mechanical prescription" (§ 30). Practical theology, in its turn, connects the work of historical theology with "the active Christian life" (§ 28), and gives philosophical theology its proper mooring in the actual experience of the Church (§§ 37-38). In this way, the theological disciplines are protected against isolation from each other, no matter how technical their work. The student, as well as the practitioner, finds it possible to view theological studies as an integrated whole.

BIBLIOGRAPHICAL NOTE

Schleiermacher's other major published works are all available in English: *The Christian Faith,* ed. by H. R. Mackintosh and J. S. Stewart (New York: Harper Torchbooks); *Christmas Eve: Dialogue on the Incarnation,* tr. by Terrence N. Tice (Richmond: John Knox Press, 1967); *On Religion: Addresses in Response to Its Cultured Critics,* tr. by Terrence N. Tice (Richmond: John Knox Press, 1969); and *Schleiermacher's Soliloquies,* tr. by Horace L. Friess (Chicago: Open Court, 1926). These are also in paperback. Other works less easily obtainable: *The Life of Schleiermacher as Unfolded in his Autobiography and Letters,* tr. by Frederica Rowan (London: Smith, Elder & Co., 1860), and *Selected Sermons of Schleiermacher,* tr. by Mary F. Wilson (London: Hodder & Stoughton, 1890).

By far the most influential interpretation of Schleiermacher in English has been that contained in H. R. Mackintosh's *Types of Modern Theology* (N. Y.: Scribner, 1937). It is unfortunately not reliable, however, at many important points. Richard R. Niebuhr's book, *Schleiermacher on Christ and Religion: A New Introduction* (N. Y.: Scribner, 1964) provides a valuable corrective. The latter shows more interest in the "style" of Schleiermacher than in specific problems of organizing theological study dealt with in the *Brief Outline.* Detailed treatment of some of these problems, especially those related to the formation of basic Christian doctrine, is given in my Princeton Theological Seminary dissertation, *Schleiermacher's Theological Method* (1961). No similarly extensive treatment of basic problems raised by the *Brief Outline* and the Introduction to *The Christian Faith* has appeared in German.

The best German text to use is Heinrich Scholz's edition: *Kurze*

Darstellung des theologischen Studiums, Kritische Ausgabe mit Einleitung und Register (Leipzig, 1910, xxxvi, 134 pp.). The index is inadequate, so has been greatly expanded in the present English edition. The latest printing of the Scholz edition omits most of his introduction, which is still useful even though his interpretation of the book needs considerable revision now (Hildesheim: G. Olms, 1961, xiv, 134 pp.).

INDEX

(Numeric references are to sections unless otherwise indicated.)